MW00425101

Small-scale Ministry Dynamics

Where The Heart of Discipleship Happens

Rev. Bob DeSagun, Ph.D.

"Who dares despise the day of small things…"
Zechariah 4:10 NIV

CONTENTS

PREFACE   1

SECTION 1 - PERSPECTIVES

CHAPTER 1
INTRODUCTION - SECTION 1   7

CHAPTER 2
ANTS, HYRAXES, LOCUSTS
AND LIZZARDS   13

CHAPTER 3
HEAD, SHOULDERS, KNEES AND TOES   19

CHAPTER 4
TWO IN THE HAND IS WORTH FIVE
IN THE BUSH   25

CHAPTER 5
SMALL IS BIG   35

CHAPTER 6
CHEESE OR NO CHEESE?   45

CHAPTER 7
STAFF, STONES, SLING AND
SHEPHERD'S BAG   51

CHAPTER 8
CONCLUSION (SECTION 1)   59

SECTION 2 - LEADERSHIP

CHAPTER 9
INTRODUCTION (SECTION 2)   69

CHAPTER 10
TWO TALENTS LEADERSHIP   75

CHAPTER 11
THE FAMILY DIMENSION   79

CHAPTER 12
PAUL'S METAPHORS   85

CHAPTER 13
THE FIVE ELEMENTS   91

CHAPTER 14
CONCLUSION (SECTION 2)   111

SECTION 3 - HEALTH

CHAPTER 15
INTRODUCTION (SECTION 3)   123

CHAPTER 16
THE VARIABLES   127

CHAPTER 17
THE TASK   133

CHAPTER 18
THE CONTEXT   139

CHAPTER 19
THE FAITHFUL   145

CHAPTER 20
THE FRUIT   153

CHAPTER 21
CONCLUSION (SECTION 3)   159

SECTION 4 - APPROACH

CHAPTER 22
INTRODUCTION (SECTION 4)   173

CHAPTER 23
GATHERING   179

CHAPTER 24
WORSHIP   185

CHAPTER 25
SERMON   191

CHAPTER 26
FOOD   199

CHAPTER 27
COMMUNITY   205

CHAPTER 28
ACCOUNTABILITY   211

CHAPTER 29
MISSIONS   215

CHAPTER 30
CONCLUSION (SECTION 4)   223

EPILOGUE   229

PREFACE

Discipleship was designed to be personal in nature. Though the mandate of Christ's Great Commission is expansive, the process of discipleship is most effectively accomplished on a small-scale. Jesus demonstrated and modeled this principle throughout His ministry on earth. He confined the bulk of His discipleship efforts on 12 men and even further focused on only three (the disciples Peter, James, and John). He knew and understood the dynamics involved in small-scale ministry that would have the greatest impact on the individuals He met with and how that would impact His discipleship efforts. Effect discipleship is done best on a small-scale because it is relational.

This book is designed to examine some of the most vital dynamics of discipleship through the lens of small-scale ministry. This book also provides some biblical and practical considerations and approaches. This book is a compilation of four separate books I authored from my small church series. Each section of this book represents the exact contents from each of the individual books. The books (now each individually transcribed in the sections of this book) were originally written with the small church in mind, but many of the principles, concepts and approaches are adaptable in any small-scale ministry context. Hence, this book is useful for small-scale ministry contexts like small groups of larger churches, care groups, leadership teams, ministry teams, chaplaincy, church governing boards, and Bible study groups.

All sections of this book were written with the popular press in mind aside from Section 2 on leadership. This section utilizes some popular press writing but reflects more of an academic and scholarly writing style because most of the material is a direct result of my doctoral dissertation on the development of a strategic approach to small church leadership.

Finally, the concepts and principles outlined in this book are never intended to criticize any other size or model of church in advocacy for the small church. The intent of this book is to encourage and equip individuals who are involved in small-scale ministry.

SECTION 1
PERSPECTIVES

From the book
DON'T SUPERSIZE IT!
10 Healthy Perspectives for the Small Church

Over half of Protestant churches in America run less than 100 people in attendance. Small churches have made up the majority of the Christian landscape for centuries, yet pastors and members of small churches commonly struggle with feelings of insecurity, insignificance and even failure because of the size of their church. They've tried everything to grow and "supersize" their church to no avail resulting only in confusion, frustration, burnout, disappointment and discouragement. Bob DeSagun shares over 12 years of experience pastoring in a small church coupled with three and a half years of doctoral study and research to provide 10 healthy perspectives designed to encourage and inspire those who pastor, serve or attend a small church.

CHAPTER 1
Introduction (Section 1)

"Supersize it!" That was a familiar phrase coined by a popular fast-food franchise about a decade ago. If you wanted to add an extra large order of French fries and an extra large soft drink to your combo meal, you would just tell them to "supersize it." As Americans faced an obesity epidemic, the fast-food chain made a strategically healthy move to simplify their menu by eliminating the option, but the phrase still remains with us today. In a culture where the notion that bigger is better, fast food customers were "supersizing" their meals to their own unhealthy demise. They were taking on more than they could chew.

I believe this concept of "supersizing" is true of many small churches; at least it was for me. Perhaps you can relate. Have you ever wished that more people attended your church? I definitely have. I wanted more people simply because I thought that it would make me look and feel more successful and significant as a pastor. If you're a pastor of a small church, you can probably relate to what I am talking about. Or maybe you attend a small church and wish your church were bigger. Perhaps you would feel you were a part of something significant if more people attended your church.

People desire to feel significant and are constantly searching for some form of it in their lives. We search for significance in our families, in our work, and in our communities. So why not in our church? For many years, I have attributed significance and worth by the size of my church. Feelings of insignificance created insecurities that haunted me as a small church pastor because my church wasn't big.

Pastors have a tendency to play the numbers game. When two pastors meet for the first time, the inevitable question will come up – How big is your church? The pastor with the bigger number trumps the other as if their church were more significant and more successful. I'm certain pastors are not the only ones who play this game. Church members play the same game. Either way, it's unhealthy.

A church's success and significance have been unfairly and superficially measured by these so-called numbers. People typically equate a large church as successful and significant and a small church as unsuccessful and insignificant. This is obviously not true, but a continual emphasis on these numbers only creates and fosters an unhealthy perspective and an inaccurate representation of church success and significance.

When I planted our church in the summer of 2002, I had dreams of becoming a megachurch. I envisioned reaching the masses for Jesus. I pictured a state-of-the-art facility working with a multi-million dollar budget. I anticipated having a variety of ministries and various outreach programs. I had a desire to lead an exemplary leadership team consisting of hundreds of committed volunteers. I imagined our church having a skilled and talented worship band led by an amazing singer songwriter who had a voice like angel. I wanted our church to have the most cutting-edge audio and video equipment. I saw myself preaching to thousands of members who were growing in their faith as committed followers of Jesus. I had a supersized vision!

I diligently worked to prepare myself for this huge role. I bought and read numerous books on church growth strategies. I read countless church growth articles. I attended and participated in various church growth conferences, seminars and workshops. You name it; I did it! After all this reading, attending and preparing, I was ready to grow my church – I was ready to supersize it!

Instead of a supersized church, our church ended up plateauing at approximately 50 people. One time, in hopes to break this plateau, I challenged our church to invite as many people they could to our next Easter service. Easter was always a great opportunity to grow a church, so we made it a goal that year to have over 100 people attend that service. The people in our church responded and rose to the challenge. The anticipation of Easter Sunday grew in excitement. We were ready! Easter Sunday was finally here, and we did it! We finally reached our goal of having over 100 people in service, but that victory was very short lived. We dwindled right back down to 50 people in service the following Sunday. What did we do wrong? Why didn't we grow? I implemented everything that I read and learned from the book authors and conference speakers. Our church was not growing. Instead, our excitement turned into confusion, frustration, disappointment and discouragement. I was ready to throw in the towel and call it quits.

I found myself so perplexed that I began to question God and started to doubt myself. I wrestled and questioned with what I was doing. Perchance, my story resonates with you or your pastor. Over the years, we applied the principles, methods and strategies taught and popularized by pastors and leaders of "successful" megachurches. The belief was that these techniques would transform our small church to eventually become like theirs – big, successful and significant. What I later discovered was that this was far from the truth. Through years of diligent prayer and tireless work, our deepest desire for a large church never came to fruition. I continued to be plagued by the insecurities that were a result of our church's lack for numerical growth. I questioned whether I was a failure as a pastor. I even questioned if our church was a failure.

These feelings, questions and struggles lead me to write this book. I hope to encourage and inspire others through what I have learned over the past 12 years of ministry experience coupled with three and half years of research in completing my doctoral degree. This book is a "small" glimpse of my passion, experience, ministry, education, and research. My aim is to provide you with ten healthy perspectives for the small church. The purpose of this book is to encourage and inspire anyone who is pastoring, serving or attending a small church.

It's time to stop supersizing your small church! It's time to stop taking on too much by trying to be a megachurch. It's time to stop trying to cram a square peg in a round hole (or in this case a large peg in a small hole). It's time to stop using large church principles, methods and strategies in the context of your unique small church ministry. Instead, it is time to start functioning the way God designed you to be as a small church.

Are you ready to stop trying to supersize your small church? Are you ready to discover what God has designed for your small church? Are you ready to be liberated? Are you ready to be free from the feelings of discouragement, disappointment and failure? Are you ready to enjoy being the small church that God created you to be? Then get ready to change your perspective and experience a healthy small church.

CHAPTER 2
Ants, Hyraxes, Locusts and Lizards

A simple Internet search will reveal that the average size church in America has less than 100 people in attendance. You'll also discover that 60 percent of Protestant churches in America run less than 100 people in attendance. Last year's annual reports from my denomination alone reflect that almost half of our 2,000 churches nationwide reported an attendance of less than 100 people. I discovered from my doctoral studies and research that a predominance of other Christian denominations are reporting similar numbers. If you pastor, serve or attend a small church, then you are considered part of the majority of churches in America. Your small church is part of the largest segment of American churches based on size.

I struggled with the thoughts of why our church wasn't growing numerically. I wrestled with the thought of being a small church. I was plagued with thoughts of failure and inadequacies because of the size of our church. I thought that it was the natural and normal thing for healthy churches to grow bigger and bigger. So when our church wasn't growing numerically, I immediately thought that there must be something wrong. Was there something wrong with me as the pastor? Was there something wrong with our church? I kept hearing stories of every other church around me that was growing. It seemed like every

13

other church around me was growing bigger and bigger while ours continued to remain small. I felt alone. Then I realized that I was not alone. There were thousands of pastors that were in my shoes - pastors who probably were struggling with the same feelings of failure and discouragement in their small churches. The fact of the matter is - we are the majority! Small churches are the majority! Could it be possible that there was something wrong with the majority of American churches? It's possible. Anything's possible. But I highly doubt it. Or could it be possible that a big part of God's plan involves a countless number of small churches? The statistics would prove that to be true.

HEALTHY PERSPECTIVE #1
Small churches make up the majority of the Christian landscape.

It came as an encouragement for me to realize that small churches make up the majority of the Christian landscape. I was finally able to entertain the possibility that there was nothing wrong with me as a pastor, and there was nothing wrong with our church being small. Just because a church is small doesn't automatically mean that something is wrong with it. Regardless of size, every church faces its own problems and issues. There is no perfect church on this side of heaven. I think too often people equate a small church to an unhealthy and unsuccessful church, and this is not true. Otherwise, we would have to conclude that over half of the churches in America are considered unhealthy. Maybe that's true, but I would think that God knows what He is doing and that there is a reason why over half of the churches in America are considered small.

Small churches each have their unique individual strengths that God uses in His redemptive plan. Proverbs 30:24-27 says, "Four things on earth are small, yet they are extremely wise: Ants are creatures of little strength, yet they store up their food in the summer; hyraxes are creatures of little power, yet they make their home in the crags; locusts have no king, yet they advance together in ranks; a lizard can be caught with the hand, yet it is found is kings' palaces." Small things are unique in their own special way. God has designed them that way for His own unique purposes. Small churches possess unique characteristics that are not only a reflection of the body of Christ but also contribute towards fulfilling the work of the Great Commission.

There are just some things that are done better on a small scale. I personally realized how advantageous being a small church is. There are several things that small churches are conveniently able to do and accomplish simply because of their size. For example, I can immediately inform all of my church members at any moment of the day by text messaging all of them in a matter of a couple of minutes. Being a mobile church (which is the case for many small churches), we can change church meeting locations last minute. As the pastor, I can be contacted by any one of my church members 24 hours a day seven days a week (I'm not sure if this is necessarily a good thing for me personally). As the pastor, I can pray for each specific individual prayer request and know whom I'm praying for. As a small church, members can invite our entire church over for dinner or social events. As a small church, our finances are freed up and unencumbered by extensive building (i.e. mortgages, utilities, water, etc.) and operational costs. And most importantly because of our size, everyone in the church actually knows one another and is able to build close, strong and meaningful relationships. This is key for discipleship. Intimacy is a key ingredient to discipleship. Intimacy promotes close, personal and meaningful relationships that are conducive for discipleship. Discipleship is most effective in small groups of people. Because of their size, small churches are advantageously poised to capitalize on this concept. Larger churches understand the need to become small through the incorporation of small groups; they understand that discipleship flourishes in intimate meaningful relationships at the small group level. This is a key advantage of small churches. British anthropologist Robin Dunbar proposed that humans could only comfortably maintain 150 stable relationships. This is referred to as Dunbar's number. Other researchers propose that the number is much smaller when you consider relationships that are close, strong, and meaningful.

Speaking of small, another interesting statistic to keep in mind is that of the megachurches. Megachurches only make up less than one-half of one percent of U.S. protestant churches. Most church growth literature and resources happen to come from megachurch pastors. Why is this? Why are small church pastors relying on this literature and on these resources that are unique to larger churches? It's because small church leaders are working off large church plans and blueprints in hopes of building larger churches, yet the two ministry contexts are uniquely different.

It is ineffective and even detrimental for small church pastors to apply larger church structures, practices, principles and strategies to the context of their small churches. The two different size churches are functionally unique and distinctive. It would be more beneficial for small churches to recognize and capitalize on their own inherent strengths rather than try and imitate larger churches. In times past, authors from larger churches have dominated church literature and resources. The purpose of this book is not only to encourage and inspire anyone who is pastoring, serving or attending a small church but also to contribute to the growing literature and resources on healthy small church ministry.

CHAPTER 3
Head, Shoulders, Knees and Toes

In 1 Corinthians 12, the apostle Paul used the human body as an analogy to illustrate the composition of the Christian church - the body of Christ. Paul explained how each part of the body is distinctively different, has unique functions, yet all work together. This analogy of the different parts of the human body not only depicts members of the church but it can also depict individual churches themselves. Each individual church is a unique, diverse, and distinctively different part of the body of Christ. We see churches that are different in denominations, ethnicities, styles, structures, and even sizes. First Corinthians 12:22-23 tells us that "…those parts of the body that seem to be weaker are indispensible, and the parts that we think are less honorable we treat with special honor." I can see how this could relate to small churches as they are perceived in the body of Christ. I'm not advocating that small churches are better than big churches; I'm arguing that the body of Christ has many different expressions as it has functions and that there is not one model of church or ministry that is considered the best. No one model, regardless of how excellent, will answer all questions, meet all needs, or solve all problems. Thinking that there is only one definitive model (or size) of church is small-minded thinking (pardon the pun). God's mission is entirely too big to be confined

19

by or able to be achieved by only one particular model of church. It is imperative that we all should remain true and never compromise the truths revealed in the Scriptures, but our approaches, models, and methodologies will vary based on context. God is trying to reach all different kinds of people; therefore, it will take all different kinds of churches working together as His body to accomplish that work.

HEALTHY PERSPECTIVE #2
Small churches are an important and necessary part in the body of Christ.

God uses every size church to fulfill His mission as we all work together as a team – large churches, medium-size churches, and small churches. Although it may appear that each church works individually, churches actually work collectively and collaboratively in the whole scheme of God's redemptive plan. Every church contributes towards completing the Great Commission through its own unique traits and strengths.

One day I received a distress call from one of my church members. Her close friend had a family member who was in critical condition as a result of a road rage incident. As this young man laid unconscious in the intensive care unit, his parents sat at his bedside in despair. The parents were young in their Christian faith. Desperate to see their son come through this horrific ordeal, they reached out to their pastor. Unfortunately, they were unable to get in contact with him, so they had another family member reach out to their pastor only to end with the same result – no contact. The parents and the other family member began to question how two separate megachurches and their pastors were not able to be contacted or able to respond to their need during such a desperate time. Their son's life was hanging in the balance, and no one was available at a moment's notice to come pray and be with them. Thankfully, one of the family members reached out to her close friend; and through this connection, I was called to aid this family. I did not know the family personally; but regardless, these folks needed some prayer and assistance. I immediately dropped what I was doing and headed to the hospital. I met my congregation member's friend who then introduced me to the parents of the boy who laid in critical condition. I spent time at the hospital praying for the boy, praying for the parents and praying with the family members who were distraught over the whole situation. The parents were very thankful that I took the time to come and be with them to pray for their son. Unfortunately, their son did not make it. Despite the outcome, I was able to be a representation of the universal church that cared so deeply for them. Eventually at a much later time, someone from the parent's megachurch was able to get in touch with the parents to pray for them as well.

I share this story to illustrate how churches work collectively and collaboratively. When one church is unavailable, another may be available; or when one church is unable, then another one will be able. The goal for all churches is to glorify God and fulfill His Great Commission. Together, churches of all sizes represent the body of Christ. This story (and this book) is not meant to bash megachurches. Every church, regardless of size, has its fair share of challenges as well as its unique strengths. One size church is not better than the other. Churches work together as one team, one body and one universal church.

In addition to working together as churches, it is important to remember that each individual member of a church plays a vital role towards the health and success of any church. The small church pastor shoulders a great deal of responsibility for the church, but the onus falls squarely upon each and every member as a whole. It is unfair to put the full blame on the pastor for what must be done cooperatively and collaboratively in the church. It doesn't matter how excellent of a leader the pastor may be, the old adage still remains to be true that "you can lead a horse to water, but you can't make him drink." The pastor is accountable to God, but every member is responsible to play his/her vital role towards the success and growth of the church. According to Ephesians 4:16, the church "…grows and builds itself up in love, as each part does its work." It is important to note that growth of the church may not necessarily be numerical. Once a church reaches its God-ordained size, then it should grow in other beneficial ways. Spiritual growth is one way and is more important than numerical growth because it is truly indicative of ministry success. Spiritual growth can be seen when people are loving God, loving one another and working towards fulfilling the Great Commission.

CHAPTER 4
Two In The Hand Is Worth Five In The Bush

There is an old proverb that says, "A bird in the hand is worth two in the bush." It teaches that we should appreciate what we have rather than what we don't have. As a small church, we should appreciate what we have. Instead of wanting something more or larger, we should appreciate and be faithful with what we have been given. God calls us to share our faith, proclaim the gospel, reach people for Jesus and make disciples. We can accomplish this with what God has given to us in our small church. Let me further illustrate this by Jesus' parable of the talents.

Jesus' parable of the talents presents some healthy perspectives for small churches. The parable in Matthew 25:14-30 illustrates the responsibility that each person has to faithfully steward the resources that God has blessed them with for the purposes of advancing His kingdom. The parable recounts three servants who are each given a number of talents (which is actually a measure of weight) by their master. The master, in return, required them to make best use of what was given to each one of them. Let's take a closer look at the parable:

> "Again, it will be like a man going on a journey, who called his servants and entrusted his wealth to them. To one he gave five bags of gold, to another two bags, and to another one bag, each according to his ability. Then he

went on his journey. The man who had received five bags of gold went at once and put his money to work and gained five bags more. So also, the one with two bags of gold gained two more. But the man who had received one bag went off, dug a hole in the ground and hid his master's money.

"After a long time the master of those servants returned and settled accounts with them. The man who had received five bags of gold brought the other five. 'Master,' he said, 'you entrusted me with five bags of gold. See, I have gained five more.'

"His master replied, 'Well done, good and faithful servant! You have been faithful with a few things; I will put you in charge of many things. Come and share your master's happiness!'

"The man with two bags of gold also came. 'Master,' he said, 'you entrusted me with two bags of gold; see, I have gained two more.'

"His master replied, 'Well done, good and faithful servant! You have been faithful with a few things; I will put you in charge of many things. Come and share your master's happiness!'

"Then the man who had received one bag of gold came. 'Master,' he said, 'I knew that you are a hard man, harvesting where you have not sown and gathering where you have not scattered seed. So I was afraid and went out and hid your gold in the ground. See, here is what belongs to you.'

"His master replied, 'You wicked, lazy servant! So you knew that I harvest where I have not sown and gather where I have not scattered seed? Well then, you should have put my money on deposit with the bankers, so that when I returned I would have received it back with interest.

"'So take the bag of gold from him and give it to the one who has ten bags. For whoever has will be given more, and they will have an abundance. Whoever does not have, even what they have will be taken from them. And throw that worthless servant outside, into the darkness, where there will be weeping and gnashing of teeth.'

From the parable, small churches can learn a lot from the servant who was given only two talents. The first lesson we can learn from the two-talent servant is that he was faithful to use what was given to him by the master, unlike the one-talent servant who did nothing. Small churches should appreciate what God has given to them (regardless of the size) and use it faithfully to advance His kingdom. Our church rents a facility on the campus of a local university. The facility has large glass windows and sliding doors that allow you to easily see into the parking lot. Practically every Sunday when church would start, I would constantly glance towards the parking lot to see who would be driving in. I was too focused on the empty seats in the church and not on the seats that had people in them. Throughout the years, I have learned to be faithful to minister to the ones who were there and not the ones who were not. Proverbs 28:20 says, "A faithful person will be richly blessed, but one eager to get rich will not go unpunished." Whether it is money or whether it is more people in our churches, an unhealthy desire for riches and increase is not without its consequences. Instead of an unhealthy desire for a bigger church, I have learned to be faithful with the gift of the small church that God had blessed me to pastor, serve and be a part of.

HEALTHY PERSPECTIVE #3
Your small church is a gift from God that should be faithfully stewarded.

The second lesson we can learn from the two-talent servant is that he was not jealous or envious of the five-talent servant. As people, we have a tendency to want more. We want more money, more recognition, more friends and more things. And when we don't have these things, we are oftentimes jealous and envious of those who do. As a small church, we are no different. We want what big churches have. We want a bigger building and a bigger budget. We want more programs and more ministries. We want more staff and more volunteers. We want more people! Small churches should neither be jealous nor envious of bigger churches because of what they have or even what they have to offer. I learned how bitter and resentful I could get when I start to envy or become jealous of the larger churches and all they had that our church didn't. Romans 13:13 says, "Let us behave decently, as in the daytime, not in carousing and drunkenness, not in sexual immorality and debauchery, not in dissention and jealousy." James 3:16 says, "For where you have envy and selfish ambition, there you find disorder and every evil practice." In Galatians

5:20, the apostle Paul list "jealousy" as one of the acts of the flesh that characterize the lives of individuals who will not inherent the kingdom of God. Paul reminds us in 1 Thessalonians 5:18 to "...give thanks in all circumstances for this is God's will for you in Christ Jesus." We should be grateful for the small church that God has us serve in. Envy and jealousy only made me ungrateful for what God has blessed, privileged and allowed me to be a part of – a wonderful small church.

HEALTHY PERSPECTIVE #4
Being jealous and envious of other churches will leave you ungrateful for what God has already blessed you with in your small church.

The third lesson we can learn from the two-talent servant is that God gave each servant according to his ability. God knows us better than we know ourselves. God knows our strengths and abilities. God knows our maximum capacity for the various aspects and areas of our lives. God knows the perfect size church for us, and sometimes that means a small church. Being a small church pastor or serving in a small church should never be viewed as a negative thing; rather, it can be a blessing in disguise. Remember that God knows all things; He could actually be saving you from unforeseen and unnecessary hardships. These are things we may not immediately perceive that God only knows.

Psalm 147:5 tells us that God's understanding is beyond measure. Proverbs 3:5 says, "Trust in the LORD with all your heart and lean not on your own understanding." We have to trust that God knows and understands what is best for us and for His kingdom. As much as we may like to pastor, serve or be part of a big church, we should be careful what we ask God for. Oftentimes not getting what we want is a hidden blessing. You don't want to bite off more than you can chew.

HEALTHY PERSPECTIVE #5
Trust that God knows more than you do and has you in a small church for His reason and purpose.

The last lesson we can learn from the two-talent servant is that he was given exactly what he needed to accomplish what his master wanted him to do. As a small church, we should trust that God has provided us with everything we need to accomplish what He'll ask us to do. If you feel you're working with limited funding, volunteers, or other resources, trust that God has given you everything you need for what He wants you to do and accomplish in and through your small church. I think that too often small churches think that "if only" they had more money, or more volunteers, or more resources that they could do more for God. As honorable as that may sound, God wants for you to trust

Him and faithfully use what you have been blessed with for His purposes.

I too fell into the trap of the "if only" mentality. I remember a time when we had thirty people in our church; and I thought "if only" we had twenty more people, we'd fill our rental space and look more like a legitimate church. So I prayed and told God that I would love to have twenty more people. As I asked God for those twenty people, I distinctly heard Him in my heart say to me, "Bob, I love those twenty people more than you would love to have them." God cared enough for those twenty people not to give them to me because He knew that I probably couldn't steward and care for them faithfully enough for His glory. As hard as it was to accept the possibility that I couldn't handle twenty more people in our church, it humbled me. God wants me to trust Him and be faithful with those He has placed under my charge and care as His undershepherd. Philippians 4:19 tells us that God will provide all of our needs. Small churches should trust that God has provided them with all they need for what He wants for them to accomplish. You have probably heard the saying, "Where God guides He provides." If God has guided us to be in a small church, then He has provided us with everything we need to accomplish what He will call us to do.

HEALTHY PERSPECTIVE #6
God has fully equipped your small church to accomplish what He'll call it to do.

Your small church is a precious gift from God. Be grateful for the wonderful fellowship that you get to be a part of. God has provided everything you'll need to accomplish exactly what He'll call your small church to do. So serve faithfully in your small church for the great reward to one day hear His voice say to you, "Well done, good and faithful servant."

CHAPTER 5
Small Is Big

On July 20, 1969, something small happened. The foot of NASA astronaut Neil Armstrong set foot on the moon. It was a small step, but that small step was big in all of history. It made history! In the eyes of Neil Armstrong, that one step was no different from the one that he took out of bed that morning. But in the eyes of historians, it was a step that made a big impact in human history. Armstrong's footprint on the lunar surface made a huge imprint on the human spirit. It was a small step that left a big footprint. There are similar small things done here on earth that are leaving big imprints in heaven. Colossians 3:2 tells us to set our minds "on things above, not on earthly things." Our focus should be on the heavenly imprints that are being made. 1 Corinthians 15:58 tells us to "Always give yourself fully to the work of the Lord, because you know that your labor in the Lord is not in vain." Small churches may do small things; but regardless of size, everything we do in the name of the Lord makes big imprints in heaven.

There are many things that small churches do that amount to big things. The problem arises when we fail to see how significant they are according to kingdom standards. It all becomes a matter of perspective. Too often we think that small things done on a small-scale really amount to nothing. Too often we think that in order to make a significant impact in the kingdom of God, it must be done on a large-scale. Our small church has done a myriad of things in the name of Christ. Together as a small church, we bought a used van for a church member in need. We were able to collect an offering just enough to help a young lady pay for funeral expenses after losing her father and brother in a tragic incident. We were able to pay a single mother's rent for a month during a financially challenging time in her life. We provided backpacks and school supplies for children of low-income families. We were able to serve a couple of hours together at a local homeless shelter and food bank. We were able to assist refugee families acclimate to American culture. We financially supported orphanages and help build homes, schools, and churches in impoverished countries around the world. We were able to financially support hurricane, tsunami, and flood victims around the world. We've helped people find employment, babysat kids, gave people rides, held the hand of a cancer survivor patient after surgery, and even taken medicine and chicken soup to those who were sick in bed. More importantly, through all of this, we were able to encourage and pray for people as they grew closer and closer to God. I'm certain that all these people that our small church was able to help will tell you that what we did for them was no small thing. And I'm certain that your small church has done similar presumably "small" things, but nothing done in the name of the Lord is considered small.

HEALTHY PERSPECTIVE #7
The presumably small things done by small churches are big when measured with kingdom standards.

We all want to be successful. We want to be successful in our careers, finances, and education. We determine success in our careers by our promotions or salaries. We determine success in our finances by how well our savings, investments portfolios, and IRAs are yielding returns. We determine success in our education by our grades or diplomas. But when it comes to ministry, what constitutes success? Is it the size of our church? Is it the size of our budget? Is it the size of our facilities? Is it the size of our programs? We know it's not, but these are some of the first things that come to mind. When we visit a megachurch, we are instantly enamored by the "bigness" of their facility. We're impressed by their polished services, the cutting edge sound of their worship "band," the eloquence of their speaker/preacher, and all the ministries and programs they offer. We may not admit it, but these are some of the things that come to mind when we think of what constitutes a successful church. Why? Because they are things that can be seen and measured. But are those things really a true measure of ministry success? What about the things that can't be seen or measured?

There are many intangible things that can neither be seen nor measured that would be a greater indication of ministry success. What I'm referring to are the intangible things of the heart that are only seen by God. In 1 Samuel 16:7, God says, "The LORD does not look at the things people look at. People look at the outward appearance, but the LORD looks at the heart." When I think of the intangible things that constitute real ministry success, I think of the single mom struggling to try to raise three kids by herself with a minimum wage job while trusting God as she faithfully gives her tithes in the offering. I think of the guy who faithfully serves in the homeless shelter every Sunday afternoon after church. I think of the grandmother who faithfully prays for her grandchildren to come to know, love and serve the Lord. I think of the couple in church that is unable to conceive children but faithfully sponsor five kids financially around the world in impoverished countries. I think of the doctor who faithfully serves overseas every summer on medical missions trips. I think of the woman with breast cancer who faithfully prays everyday for her healing as her health continues to deteriorate yet her faith continues to grow stronger and stronger. I can continue to give you countless examples of "intangibles" that far outweigh the common tangibles we typically use to define or determine ministry success. I'm certain that these are all examples of similar things that are happening in your small church as well.

HEALTHY PERSPECTIVE #8
There are numerous intangible things that cannot be measured that are greater determinants of the health and success of your small church.

I remember my ordination interview. I felt like young Anakin Skywalk before the Jedi Council answering a myriad of theological and doctrinal questions that would eventually determine whether I would be accepted into the elite Jedi Order of the ordained. For each question that was asked of me by the council, I was expected to substantiate my answers with at least two Scriptures along with their scriptural addresses. I was nervous! Other than the numerous theological and doctrinal questions that were asked of me, I remember one question in particular: How do you define "success" in ministry? I responded by referring to Jesus' parable of the talents in Matthew 25 and simply replied with one word - faithfulness. God has given each of us "talents" in the form of money, possessions, time, health, skills, or whatever else you could possibly imagine. God calls us to faithfully steward these talents for His glory until He returns. Faithfully stewarding these talents causes eternal and everlasting results in heaven that are difficult, if not impossible, to see or measure here on earth. Ministry success is determined by the things that are built upon the foundation of Christ that will last for all eternity. First Corinthians 3:11-15 says:

> For no one can lay any foundation other than the one already laid, which is Jesus Christ. If anyone builds on this foundation using gold, silver, or costly stones, wood, hay, or straw, their work will be shown for what it is, because the Day will bring it to light. It will be revealed with fire, and the fire will test the quality of each person's work. If what has been built survives, the builder will receive a reward. If it is burned up, the builder will suffer loss but yet will be saved – even though only as one escaping through the flames.

The real evidences of ministry success are the intangible things that are unseen and will be tested and determined in glory. 2 Corinthians 4:18 tells us to "fix our eyes not on what is seen, but what is unseen, since what is seen is temporary, but what is unseen is eternal." These eternal results are the true measure of ministry success. These results can only be accomplished when we trust God and are faithful to do what He asks of us for His glory.

Oftentimes in the past, I considered myself a failure as a pastor because I was unable to grow my church. Just because a church is small doesn't make it unhealthy. In the same breath, just because a church is large doesn't make it healthy either. The size of a church is not a clear indicator of whether a pastor or the church is considered successful or not. We put too much stock in numbers and size. We have become conditioned and programmed by a culture that oftentimes tells us that bigger is better. Some may argue that healthy things grow. I agree that healthy things grow, but oftentimes there is a limit to its growth. For example, a healthy person will grow to a certain height, some to six feet tall and others to only five feet two inches (like myself). But after we reach a certain height, we tend grow in other ways. There is an unhealthy obsession with pastors trying to grow their churches. In Matthew 16:18, Jesus said, "...I will build my church." The apostle Paul tells us in 1 Corinthians 3:6 that God causes the growth. Our focus should be on church health, and we should leave the growing to God. If God wants to increase the number of people that attend your church, then He will; but if He doesn't, for whatever reasons, then He won't. That doesn't excuse us from doing our part to faithfully work towards fulfilling the Great Commission.

There will even be times when a church will decrease in size, but this does not necessarily indicate that it is unhealthy or unsuccessful. Remember the story of Gideon in Judges 7 when the Lord God dwindled Gideon's army from 32,000 men to only 300? God had a purpose to decrease the number of Gideon's army for His glory. It's possible that God will decrease the size of your church for His purpose and glory. It is our job to trust Him as Gideon did despite the numbers.

Numbers should not be the one indicative factor that determines ministry success or health. The church's annual report should not dictate whether or not you have been successful as a pastor or as a church. Our church is part of a denomination that submits an annual report that consists primarily of numbers (i.e. current members, decisions for Christ, baptisms, financials, etc.). Recently our denomination added a "Going Deeper" component to the annual report that is designed to analyze and facilitate discussions behind the numbers. It is used as a tool to uncover the meaningful stories and testimonies that account for real success. I'm certain that you can personally recall several success stories from your small church that cannot be measured by numbers. Don't get me wrong, I do understand how and what these numbers have the potential to represent and measure, but I think we put too much emphasis on these numbers to the demise of small churches simply because their numbers are respectively small. These numbers have an unhealthy and discouraging way to paint a negative portrait of a small church that is not indicative of what is truly going on.

CHAPTER 6
Cheese Or No Cheese?

In 1948, Harry and Esther Snyder started a drive-thru hamburger stand in Baldwin Park, California and set out to do one thing – to take pride in all that they do to deliver only the freshest, highest quality foods and superior services at all times to their customers.[1] Now, with 281 locations in five different states, In-N-Out Burger continues to successfully operate on the basis of "simplicity" by offering only three hamburger varieties: the plain hamburger, the cheeseburger, and the "Double-Double" (a double meat patty hamburger with double cheese). You won't find chicken nuggets on the menu. You won't find tacos or burritos on the menu either. Neither will you find breakfast sandwiches nor dessert items. At In-N-Out Burger, you'll basically find one main item on the menu – burgers – and the only option you have is to have it with or without cheese. The thing about In-N-Out Burger is that their burgers are absolutely delicious! That's because they focus on doing one thing – and that's making the best burger. I'm certain that if you fill out a comment/suggestion card and ask them to carry a variety of other menu items, you'll most likely get an emphatic "no" from their decision makers. They know what they're doing, and they also know what they're not doing. They make burgers – and they're good at it!

Being a small church is very similar. God has created your small church for a specific kingdom purpose, and that is for you as a church to discover. When you discover what God has asked you to do (and only do), you'll be able to give Him your very best focused effort. Instead of imitating a large church by creating and offering several different ministries and outreach programs, ask God to reveal to you what is the one (or two) things you do well and focus on doing only those things.

When I started our church in the summer of 2002, I strived to create and offer various ministries as well as discipleship and outreach programs like all the larger churches offered. We were saying "yes" to every single person who wanted to start a different ministry in and through the church. We thought that this was a great way and opportunity to grow our church. We did worship to grow the church. We did children's ministry to grow the church. We did prayer ministry to grow the church. We did tech crew (audio and visual) ministry to grow the church. We did college ministry to grow the church. What we came to realize was that by trying to create and maintain these various ministries and programs, we spread our church leadership team extremely thin, which eventually resulted in burnout, frustration, disappointment and discouragement.

In our discovery of who we were as a small church, we came to discover what God was asking us to do all along. We kept ministry simple. By keeping

ministry simple, it kept us focused as a church –
focused on doing one (or two) things well. When we
discovered what those things were, it was easy to say
"no" to everything else. Earlier when we were saying
"yes" to start up ministries just to start ministries, we
were actually saying "no" to the very things God was
actually asking us to do and focus on instead. So now
by saying "no" to everything else, we can say "yes" to
what God is actually asking us to do. The thing that
God was asking us to do was the thing we wanted to be
the best in the world at doing. We now wanted to be
the small church that was the best in the world at doing
that. What is that? That is something you'll have to
discover for your own small church in your own unique
context. And when you discover what "that" is, you'll
be able to be focused to become the best at it.

As tempting as it is to have all the wonderful
ministries and outreach programs that larger churches
have, your best bet is to say "no" to those things and
stay focused on doing the one or two things well that
God is calling you to do. In Luke 10 when Martha was
preoccupied with the many things at hand, she asked
Jesus to tell Mary to help her. Jesus replied, "...you are
worried and upset about many things, but few things are
needed – or indeed only one. Mary has chosen what is
better, and it will not be taken away from her." I have
learned that as a small church, it is better for us to do
one or two things well rather than to do several things
mediocre or even poorly. When you discover your

unique strengths as a small church in your particular context of ministry, it will empower you to not only stay focused but also prevent you from overextending yourself.

HEALTHY PERSPECTIVE #9
Small churches should focus on doing one or two things really well rather than trying to do several things mediocre or even poorly.

As a small church, be the best small church at what you do. Don't try and do everything. Even Jesus gave His disciples only two commands – to love God and love others. Discover how you can uniquely accomplish the mandate of the Great Commission through the unique strengths of your small church. Focus all of your time, energy and resources on that one or two things your church does really well. Trust that God will use the things you do well to reach the people He wants you to reach. Fight off the temptation to be like a large church that is capable of doing a lot more. Be wise and courageous to say "no" to the things that do not employ your unique strengths and say "yes" to the things that do. Know what God has called you to do and stay focused to be the best at it.

CHAPTER 7
Staff, Stones, Sling and Shepherd's Bag

Sunday November 11, 2012 was the day when ministry in the small church began to change for the better. The day prior, I hosted a prayer breakfast at my home for any church member who wanted a free home cooked breakfast and a little piece of my heart. Almost everyone from our church showed up that morning. Following breakfast, I shared my heart and thoughts on how I felt the Holy Spirit was leading me as their pastor. I shared a little bit of my frustrations, disappointments and discouragement of trying to grow the church. I shared how I came to a place in my life that I thought I would never find myself – a place where I considered quitting the pastorate and doing something entirely different. I also shared my heart and resolve to simply and wholeheartedly follow the Lord in whatever He wanted me to do. I shared with them how I felt the Lord leading us as a church. I received a unanimous response back from those in attendance to be obedient to whatever God was asking of me and that they would support my decision. So the next morning at church, I briefly preached from the passage out of 1 Samuel 17:38-40:

> Then Saul dressed David in his own tunic. He put a coat of armor on him and a bronze helmet on his head. David fastened on his sword over the tunic and tried walking around, because he was not used to them.

"I cannot go in these," he said to Saul, "because I am not used to them." So he took them off. Then he took his staff in his hand, chose five smooth stones from the stream, put them in the pouch of his shepherd's bag and, with his sling in his hand, approached the Philistine.

In my sermon, I explained to the church how Saul's coat of armor, helmet, and sword was too big and encumbering for David to effectively operate in. I further explained how this served as an analogy of what I felt we had been doing as a church. We had been trying to wear armor and a helmet as well as wield a sword that was not only too big for us but not designed for us. I also explained how David remained true to himself when he took off Saul's coat of armor and went into battle with Goliath trusting God with what he had – a staff, stones, a sling and his shepherd's bag.

Afterwards, I briefly shared with the church how I felt that we were doing a lot of things that the Lord was not asking us to do. We were doing things and running ministry programs that you'll typically find in any other church – good things. I explained that these typical ministry things that we had been doing was kind of expected of us as a church to do. It was like Saul offering this armor to David to fight Goliath – it was expected that a warrior would know to wear armor and be capable of wielding a sword in order to do well in battle. But instead, David recognized that it wasn't him, and according to the Scriptures, he "took them off." I explained to the church that I felt that we had been trying to act and function like a big church using big church programs and big church structures when all the while we were just a small church. In doing so, we had not only burned out our leadership team but also discouraged the people with a (false) sense of failure in our lack of numerical growth. We were not a big church, and we may never become a big church – and that was ok for us. Our goal from that day forward was to be true to who God had created us to be and simply act and operate in such a manner.

HEALTHY PERSPECTIVE #10
Stop imitating larger churches and be the small church that God has called and created it to be.

So that morning, we did exactly what David did with Saul's armor - we "took them off". This phrase "took them off" comes from the Hebrew word *sur*, which means to "put aside." We put aside ministries, programs, and structures that were not characteristic of us as a small church. That morning I announced that I was relieving all ministry leaders – prayer ministry, worship ministry, children's ministry, administrative support ministry, tech crew (our audio/visual set-up/break-down ministry), and missions ministry. We put aside all these things that had been encumbering us, and we started over from scratch.

We started with worship. I picked up my guitar (mindful that I had just relieved the worship leader and her team) and led the church in worship. I led them using Matt Redman's song "Heart of Worship." Before I did, I shared with the church the story behind this particular song. If you don't know the story, let me recount it for you in the words of Matt Redman himself from his book *Unquenchable Worshipper: Coming Back to the Heart of Worship*:

A few years back in our church, we realized some of the things we thought were helping us in our worship were actually hindering us. They were throwing us off the scent of what it means to really worship. We had always set aside lots of time in our meetings for worshipping God through music. But it began to dawn on us that we'd lost something. The fire that used to characterize our worship had somehow grown cold. In some ways, everything looked great. We had some wonderful musicians, and a good quality sound system. There were lots of new songs coming through, too. But somehow we'd started to rely on these things a little too much, and they'd become distractions. Where once people would enter in no matter what, we'd now wait to see what the band was like first, how good the sound was, or whether we were 'into' the songs chosen.

Mike, the pastor, decided on a pretty drastic course of action: we'd strip everything away for a season, just to see where our hearts were. So the very next Sunday when we turned up at church, there was no sound system to be seen, and no band to lead us. The new approach was simple - we weren't going to lean so hard on those outward things any more. Mike would say, 'When you come through the doors of the church on Sunday, what are you bringing as your offering to God? What are you going   to   sacrifice   today?'

If I'm honest, at first I was pretty offended by the whole thing. The worship was my job! But as God softened my heart, I started to see His wisdom all over these actions. At first the meetings were a bit awkward: there were long periods of silence, and there wasn't too much singing going on. But we soon began to learn how to bring heart offerings to God without any external trappings we'd grown used to. Stripping everything away, we slowly started to rediscover the heart of worship.

After a while, the worship band and the sound system re-appeared, but now it was different. The songs of our hearts had caught up with the songs of our lips.

Out of this season, I reflected on where we had come to as a church, and wrote this song:

When the music fades,
All is stripped away,
And I simply come;
Longing just to bring something that's of worth
That will bless Your heart.

I'll bring You more than a song,
For a song in itself
Is not what You have required.
You search much deeper within
Through the way things appear;
You're looking into my heart.

In the chorus I tried to sum up where we were at with worship:

I'm coming back to the heart of worship,
And it's all about You,
All about You, Jesus.
I'm sorry, Lord, for the thing I've made it,
When it's all about You,
All about You, Jesus. [2]

We were brought back to the heart of worship – it was all about Jesus. Maybe somewhere for us it had been about something else. Maybe it was to build a bigger church. Whatever it was, it was "put aside" and replaced with what really mattered – Jesus. When we rediscovered Jesus through hearts of worship, we came to see who we were in Him. Discovering God became a discovery of ourselves and of our church.

That day we became true to God, to ourselves, and to our church. We came to realize that it was no longer about what we wanted to be but rather what God wanted us to be. Instead of doing this and doing that (all the things you would expect a church to do), it became a matter of discovering who we were in Christ and enjoying our special place in the body of Christ as a small church. We let go of the pursuit to become a big church and simply celebrated who we were as a small church.

I will confess, there are times when I'm tempted to revisit the old thoughts of growing a bigger church. I see and hear the things that the larger churches are doing, and I start to become envious and jealous. That's when I have to remind myself of the uniqueness that God created and designed us to be. The apostle Paul understood this in 1 Corinthians 15:9-11 when he wrote, "For I am the least of the apostles and do not even deserve to be called an apostle, because I persecuted the church of God. But by the grace of God I am what I am..." Maybe you felt like Paul did. Maybe you felt that your church was the least of all churches, and maybe you felt that it didn't even deserve to be called a church because of its size. Your church is what it is – a small church by the grace of God.

God has designed your church to be what it is. Just like the way He created people. Some are black, some are white, and some are Asian; some are tall and some are short; some are extroverts while others are introverts; some are fast and others are slow; some are thin while others are fuller; some are brunettes and some are (naturally) blonde. We need to discover and remind ourselves how special and unique in God's eyes we are and be true to ourselves and to Him.

When a person or a church discovers who they are in Christ, they can be free from the pressures of becoming anything else. It no longer becomes a matter of "doing" but rather "being." When we accepted who we were in Christ – in our case a small church – we were liberated from the pressures of trying to become something that we were not meant to be or accomplish something we were never meant to do. If you're a doctor, you're not expected to change or repair a carburetor. If you're an accountant, you're not expected to extract a decayed molar. If you're a fireman, you're not expected to teach high school math. Who you are will determine what you are capable of doing as well as what you should be doing. Being acutely aware of who or what God created you to be will empower you to accomplish what He will ask you to do.

CHAPTER 8
Conclusion (Section 1)

Your small church is part of God's plan to reach people with the life-changing message of the gospel of Jesus Christ. Your small church is not only significant but also vital in the fulfillment of The Great Commission. God has placed you in that small church for His reasons and His purposes.

Whether you pastor, serve or attend a small church, the unique role that you play is critical and essential for your church to grow. Growing spiritually healthy is much more important than growing numerically. A church that is growing spiritually healthy is a church whose members are obedient to God as a reflection of their growing love for Him that results in a growing love for others. It is a church that is committed towards fulfilling The Great Commission. Your church will grow when each member does its part faithfully.

A good-natured congregation member of mine once told me years ago that we need to start acting like and big church in order to become a big church. In essence, she wanted to supersize the church, and so did I. Year after year we acted like a big church but never saw the numerical growth. Instead we ended up with a burned out, confused, discouraged and disappointed church with a pastor who was ready to quit. But seeing our small church through these perspectives has renewed and reinvigorated my passion and excitement again for ministry.

My prayer is that these 10 healthy perspectives for your small church will encourage and inspire you to be the best small church that God has called you to be. Don't try and imitate larger churches by taking on way too much for your own good. Instead of trying to be a big church, be a healthy church and don't supersize it.

ENDNOTES
Section 1

1. Adapted from In-N-Out Burger's website www.in-n-out.com
2. Matt Redman, *The Unquenchable Worshipper: Coming Back to the Heart of Worship* (Ventura, CA: Regal Books, 2001).

SECTION 2
LEADERSHIP

From the book
TWO TALENTS LEADERSHIP
A Strategic Small Church Leadership Approach

In a culture where the notion that bigger has oftentimes been mistakenly considered better, small church pastors are relentlessly trying to increase the size of their churches. In an attempt to grow their churches, they have adopted popular leadership paradigms designed by larger churches that may be unsuitable to their unique small church ministry context. In this book, Bob DeSagun provides small church pastors with a more suitable leadership resource. He proposes a strategic small church leadership approach that is a result of 13 years of experience pastoring a small church coupled with three and a half years of doctoral study and research in the field of ecclesial leadership. The principles of his Two Talents Leadership approach outlined in this book is a product of his doctoral dissertation work.

CHAPTER 9
Introduction (Section 2)

Statistics continue to affirm that a vast majority of Christian churches are considered small in size and is indicative of where most Christian pastors will end up serving. Yet amidst these statistics, the Christian market still remains flooded with literature and resources on leadership models and ministry strategies designed for larger churches that are either inadequate or unsuitable for the small church. It's not that these resources are not helpful but rather some of the concepts and principles from these resources are being applied by small church pastors to their church's detriment and demise. In my first book *Don't Supersize It! 10 Healthy Perspectives for the Small Church*, I mention how ineffective and even detrimental it is for small church pastors to apply larger church structures, practices and strategies to the context of their small church ministry simply because the two contexts are functionally different.[1]

General principles of leadership are applicable to all contexts, but specific methodologies and approaches are necessary to suit each unique context. To suggest that there is one universal leadership approach suitable and effective for all leadership contexts is preposterous. In his book *Leading With Cultural Intelligence: The Real Secret To Success*, author David Livermore states, "Many leadership and management books give us the idea that leadership is a universal skill set that works the same anywhere. It sounds promising, but it just doesn't jive with the realities of leading in today's multifaceted, globalized world."[2] The contemporary Christian church has grown to become multifaceted and global and engages ministry in a variety of contexts. As a former officer in the United States Marine Corps, I understood that I was expected to uphold foundational leadership traits like courage, honesty, integrity, and sacrifice. These qualities and traits are expected of all military leaders. But based on my military occupational specialty as an aircraft maintenance officer for a helicopter squadron, the strategic scheduling of maintenance personnel, supplies, parts and work was critical for the operational readiness and success of our squadron. The officer in charge of a military supply warehouse that maintains and issues equipment or even the officer in charge of a platoon, company, or battalion that leads Marines into the front lines of combat will each demand and require a uniquely tailored leadership approach for their distinct operational context. The leadership approach that I suggest in this book is no different. The small church leadership approach that I propose does not deny the universal biblical attributes and qualifications for Christian leaders outlined in the Books of 1 Timothy and Titus. Being trustworthy, above reproach, faithful, temperate, self-controlled, respectable, hospitable, gentle and reputable are all biblically foundational qualities for Christian leaders. This small church leadership approach not only advocates for these foundational biblical qualities but also originates from a biblically historical framework. It is also important to note that this approach that I propose for small churches is "an" approach and not "the" approach.

The development of a biblically value-laden approach that is specifically and distinctively germane and contextual towards leadership for the small church is long overdue. The strategic leadership approach that I present in this book is a direct result of not only my experience as a small church pastor but also my formal doctoral education that includes study and research – it is a direct reflection of my doctoral dissertation. The purpose of my dissertation was to explore biblical values from the Christian sacred text of 1 Thessalonians 2 verses 7-8 and 11-12 and examine how they can contribute towards an understanding and development of a strategic small church leadership approach. The findings of the study serve to provide the basis of the principles and concepts outlined in this leadership approach.

Leadership continues to be a growing field of interest for the Christian church. In his book *Leading Organizations: Perspectives For A New Era*, editor Gill Robinson Hickman states, "Assessing the environment and adapting the organization to changes in context are essential components of leadership in new era organizations."[3] It is imperative for pastors and church leaders to consider leadership approaches that are not merely popular but prove efficacious for their distinctively unique ministry context. Based on the statistics that continue to affirm that the majority of the Christian landscape is made up of small churches, the need for and development of strategic small church leadership approaches are not only evident and necessary but also vital to the efficacy and success of the global Christian church towards fulfilling the Great Commission.

CHAPTER 10
Two Talents Leadership

In one of the chapters from my first book, I share four healthy perspectives for the small church from Jesus' parable in Matthew 25:14-30 from the viewpoint of the servant who received two talents. The first healthy perspective that we can learn from the parable is to realize that our small church is a gift from God that should be faithfully stewarded.[4] The second healthy perspective is not to be jealous and envious of other churches that will leave us ungrateful for what God has already blessed us with in our small church.[5] The third healthy perspective is to trust that God knows more than we do and has us in a small church for His reason and purpose.[6] And the fourth healthy perspective from the parable that we can learn from the servant who received two talents is that God has fully equipped our small church to accomplish what He'll call it to do.[7] In the parable, the distinctly unique position of the servant who had received the two talents is the overarching premise for the title of this book and this unique strategic leadership approach for small churches.

I have coined the term "two talents leadership" to describe a ministry leadership context that intertwines God's divine providence with a servant leader's faithful stewardship - it is about how a servant leader faithfully stewards a small measure compared to a large one. In this particular case, it is intended to describe small church pastors as oppose to large church pastors. Two talents leadership is about small church leadership.

Two talents leadership is understood in the context of having received from God a smaller measure. In Jesus' parable, one servant received five talents while another received only two. This is comparable to how one pastor has been given responsibility over a large church while another may have been given responsibility over a small church - the five talents indicative of the large church while the two talents indicative of the small church. This is wholly contingent upon God's divine providence. Only God determines who will pastor a large church and who will pastor a small church. We must trust God's sovereignty and knowledge regarding the number of people or the size of church we have been entrusted to pastor.

Two talents leadership predisposes the concept of faithful stewardship above all else. The concept focuses not on what we don't have but rather on what we do. It doesn't focus on what we wished we had but on what God has already blessed us with. Stewardship is not about God withholding from us but instead about God giving to us. The concept of two talents leadership elucidates how God is the owner and we are merely managers of His resources and blessings. God has absolute ownership rights to all things. Psalm 24:1 says, "The earth is the LORD's, and the fullness

thereof, the world and those who dwell therein..."
Stewardship is faithfully using all that God has entrusted to us for His purposes and glory. In his book *The Strategically Small Church*, author Brandon O'Brien explained how, "The congregations that made up the early Christian church didn't have the impressive presence many ministries have today through television, radio, and the Internet. They didn't have campuses and facilities and programs. They didn't have educated clergy. God used the combined faithfulness and strength of dozens of under-resourced, poorly staffed, badly programmed, and unprofessional small churches to change the world forever. All they had was the gospel of Christ and the Holy Spirit. That was plenty to expand the kingdom of God across the entire world. This is plenty still today."[8]

Stewardship has never been about what we do not have but about what we do have and how we use it faithfully for the interest of God and His kingdom. Two talents leadership is about leadership in the small church and how to effectively utilize and maximize available resources that will advance the kingdom of God. Though the concept of two talents leadership derives from the premise of having received a smaller measure, its emphasis is never on the amount but rather on the handling – the faithful stewardship of. The point of two talents leadership is never a matter of how much we have been given but rather how well we use what we have been given.

CHAPTER 11
The Family Dimension

It is no surprise that the first century Christian church was made up of small congregations as oppose to the larger and megachurch congregations that we see today. It is apparent from the Scriptures that the gathering of the early Christian believers in homes could not possibly accommodate large gatherings. These home gatherings are mentioned in Acts 1:13 where the disciples met in the upper room of a house; in Acts 12:2 where believers gathered and were praying at Mary's house; in Acts 16:40 where believers gathered at Lydia's house for encouragement. There is also the mention of the church in Priscilla and Aquila's house in Romans 16 verses 3 and 5; the church in Nympha's house in Colossians 4:15; as well as the church that met in Philemon and Apphia's house in Philemon 1-2. The early first century Christian gatherings were small in nature simply because they met in houses. In his book *Introducing Early Christianity: A Topical Survey of Its Life, Beliefs & Practices*, author and lecturer Laurie Guy explained that early first century Christian meetings in homes fostered multiple meeting sites in any one city and that "excavations of wealthy first-century homes in Corinth had an *atrium* (central court) averaging 55 square meters and a *triclinium* (dining room) averaging 36 square meters" allowing no more than 50 people to meet in one home.[9] Guy also explained how the home settings of the New Testament church "fostered the relational dimension of the faith."[10] In his article entitled "Sacred Space, The Arts and Theology: Some Light From History," R. Kevin Seasoltz explained that the early Christians would gather and worship in private homes because households constituted the basic organizational structure in the early church.[11] Since its inception, the house churches of the New Testament appeared to be a deliberate apostolic pattern conducive for relational discipleship through the structure of the family.

The small church has a distinct advantage for relational discipleship in its inherent family dimension. In his book *The New Conspirators: Creating The Future One Mustard Seed At A Time,* author Tom Sine explained how the early church was "a new family who embodied a whole new way of being that was clearly counter to every culture in which they found themselves."[12] In his article "Christian Family Life: Some Pastoral Priorities," Brian Hearne explained how the small Christian community can be seen as the ecclesial extended family, "where the bond of grace sets up not only new relationships but also new kinship patterns, transcending ethnic, national and racial barriers."[13] According to O'Brien, as people become more transient in their geographical move farther away from their biological family, people of all ages have benefitted from churches that function as a family.[14] O'Brien further explained that there has been an increasing trend among young adults who are looking for a church that can offer them an experience of becoming part of a family.[15] The family structure of the early Christian church lends to the distinct and unique advantage possessed by the contemporary small church towards relational discipleship. One of the greatest inherent strengths of the small church is its family dimension; and as O'Brien aptly states, "Despite the difficulties, learning to understand the church as family will be profoundly rewarding. In fact, I am convinced that if the small church had no other inherent value, no other particular strength, this one thing would make it a strategic tool for the future of the Christian faith."[16]

Churches throughout America typically operate in some corporate structural manner. There are board meetings, protocols, policies, business and financial reports, corporate structure and programs – and all of this is necessary for the most part. It is essential for large churches to operate in such a fashion by employing corporate structure and procedures to accommodate the various and diverse ministries, outreach and discipleship programs as well as manage facilities, staff and volunteers. Pastors and leaders in large churches tend to operate more along the lines of administrators – administrators of structure, policies, programs, funds and even people. It becomes practically necessary to operate in such a manner due to the large amounts of resources that need to be properly managed and maintained. Small churches, on the other hand, are uniquely situated in a way to avoid having to operate in such a corporate manner. Like the early New Testament churches, small churches are situated uniquely to function as a family. In their book *Small Is Big: Unleashing the Big Impact of Intentionally Small Churches*, church planters Tony and Felicity Dale along with George Barna founder of the Barna Group state, 'If we think that "big is beautiful" when it comes to church, then we will tend to have a more corporate structure, as oppose to small groups that operate like family.'[17]   Larger churches offer small groups to compensate for the lack of intimacy and relational dynamics that is oftentimes not conducive in their larger gatherings and services. This is why the small church by nature is advantageously situated for fostering intimacy and relationships conducive for discipleship.

God's church was designed to be family dimensional. Ephesians 2:19 tells us that we are "members of the household of God." The family dimensionality of Christ's church is a result of communion and fellowship inherent in our DNA. God designed for us to live in community. We see this concept epitomized in the Holy Trinity: God the Father, Son, and Holy Spirit existing together in a unique fellowship. The Persons of the Trinity are distinguished by family relational roles and titles (i.e.

Father and Son). Family is at the core of God's design for church.

In a society where families are oftentimes broken and dysfunctional, the church ought to serve as an extended family bringing God's love, care, healing and redemption to the lives of individuals who are desperately searching for a place to belong. Christ's church is created to function in this unique role to embrace and welcome those whom our Heavenly Father will call into His eternal family. Because of its size, the small church is uniquely positioned to foster the intimacy necessary to create a genuine family environment where people know, love, and care for one another. Livermore states that "the family system is widely regarded as the single most important cultural system leaders need to understand."[8] It is important for small church pastors to understand the significance of the function and dynamics of family. Small church pastors can leverage this understanding of family towards the development and employment of a strategic small church leadership approach.

CHAPTER 12
Paul's Metaphors

Metaphors are powerful figures of speech that assist in providing insight and understanding into an author's thoughts and ideas. Author and professor Timothy Laniak explained in his book *Shepherds After My Own Heart: Pastoral Traditions and Leadership in the Bible* that, "Because of this natural, conceptualizing movement from the known to the unknown, a majority of metaphors make use of concrete or physical realities to describe less tangible realities."[19] Laniak further explained that "While many metaphors are much more modest in their aims, they all have a capacity to communicate in ways that are unique to figurative language. They are compact, felicitous and engaging. They prompt reflection, feeling, evaluation and action. The meaning of a metaphor, like the meaning of a joke, can be unpacked and, to a certain extent, explained. But the full impact of the image on one's imagination requires an image. Metaphors are irreducible moments of multi-modal communication."[20] Biblical writers used metaphors as strategic rhetorical devices to bring greater clarity and understanding to their thoughts and ideas.

Early first century Christian communities were greatly influenced by the family as a framework to adopt a form and style of leadership that was applicable to its particular context and circumstance. In his book

A Pauline Theology of Church Leadership, Andrew Clarke explained that the household setting for the early Christian communities provided models for leadership structures where heads of households became the overseer of a local Christian house church, but the household was also a key Pauline metaphor for his conception of the church and for its leadership.[21] And in his book *Serve the Community of the Church: Chrisitans As Leaders and Ministers,* Clarke also asserted that the family was a metaphor that was occasionally applied to the church and "may well have provided for some the most appropriate context for considering the nature and pattern for organizing the local Christian community and defining its leadership."[22]

In 1 Thessalonians 2 verses 7-8 and 11-12, the apostle Paul utilized the metaphorical images of "mother" and "father" in addressing the small Christian community in Thessalonica. The use of these particular metaphors was not only a strategic appeal to his Thessalonian audience but also a framework for his intentional leadership approach. Let's take a look at the passage in 1 Thessalonians 2 verses 7-8 and 11-12:

> But we were gentle among you, like a nursing mother taking care of her own children. So, being affectionately desirous of you, we were ready to share with you not only the gospel of God but also our own selves, because you had become very dear to us...For you know how, like a father with his children, we exhorted each one of you and encouraged you and charged you to walk in a manner

worthy of God, who calls you into his own kingdom and glory.

1 Thessalonians is a letter written by the apostle Paul to the early Christian believers in the city of Thessalonica. In this letter, Paul reestablishes his prior connections in the city despite the geographical and physical distance between them. Paul made his initial visit to Thessalonica with Silas where they made a group of converts to the Christian faith with the hospitality of Jason (Acts 17:7). Paul was later forced to leave (1 Thessalonians 2:17) in a hasty and untimely fashion (Acts 17:5-10). It was in Corinth that Paul wrote his first letter carried by Timothy to the fledgling church in Thessalonica. Paul's letter to the Thessalonians carried with it encouragement amidst their afflictions from outsiders whom were pressuring them to turn from Christianity and turn back to their previous way of living.

The text of 1 Thessalonians 2 verses 7-8 and 11-12 appears apologetic in nature, but many contemporary interpreters suggest that the apostle Paul had another underlying motive. The initial and commonly interpreted premise of the text was that Paul was defending himself to his Thessalonian audience from those whose aim was to discredit both him and his teachings, but some contemporary interpreters have not discounted that Paul was also appealing to his audience as well. In his article entitled, "Infants, Nursing Mother, and Father: Paul's Portrayal of a Pastor,"

Jeffrey Weima posited that Paul's primary function of the text was to defend himself, but a secondary function of parenetic or hortatory nature was also present. It is in this secondary function that the metaphorical images of both mother and father illustrate the roles pastors and ecclesial leaders play in their congregations.[23] Paul was appealing to his audience utilizing a leadership approach that was parental in nature.

In this passage, the apostle Paul likens himself to that of a mother and a father. Paul further accentuates his leadership character by espousing five distinctive traits familiar with the contextual institutional roles and responsibilities of Jewish parents in first-century Mediterranean. In his article, Weima further examined the metaphors from 1 Thessalonians 2:1-12 to suggest that the images capture the role of pastors and how they ought to think of themselves as well as how they ought to act within their congregations.[24] Understanding the roles and responsibilities of first century parents in the Mediterranean is an insightful approach to Pauline leadership that is relationally applicable towards the development of a strategic approach to small church leadership.

The apostle Paul's metaphorical use of the mother and father images not only generalized the subsequent character traits displayed by him to his Thessalonian audience but also characterized his particular leadership approach. The descriptors used by the apostle Paul from each parental metaphor evoke familiar Christian subcultural traditions that were initially established by Jesus Christ and passed on in the teachings of the apostles. In his book *A Spiritual Theology of the Priesthood: The Mystery of Christ and the Mission of the Priest*, Dermot Power explained how Paul modeled Christ to the early Christian communities of the New Testament in his display of pastoral love.[25] The five traits espoused by Paul in 1 Thessalonians 2 verses 7-8 and 11-12 depict not only his contextual leadership approach but also the embodiment of Christ's character. These character traits espoused by Paul encapsulate the five foundational elements of this particular strategic leadership approach for small churches.

CHAPTER 13
The Five Elements

Cultural elements from the passage of 1 Thessalonians 2 verses 7-8 and 11-12 hold a deeper understanding to the apostle Paul's leadership approach to the small Christian community in Thessalonica. Vernon Robbins developed a unique method of interpretation known as *sociorhetorical criticism* that brings together social–scientific and literary–critical approaches to explore early Christianity. Robbins explained that sociorhetorical criticism integrates strategies and techniques used among various literary, social, cultural, and ideological interpreters in an integrated, rhetorical system of analysis and interpretation. Robbins denied that there is only one valid way of interpretation and investigated Christianity as a cultural phenomenon and treated its canonical texts as ideological constructs. Robbins explored the relation of texts to society and culture utilizing multiple methods of interpretation in an organized and programmatic way that provided distinctly new insights into the development of early Christianity. In his book entitled *The Tapestry of Early Christian Discourse: Rhetoric, Society, and Ideology*, Robbins explained how sociorhetorical criticism "invites interpreters to explore a wide arrange of textures through a process of creating and dismantling various boundaries to create arenas of understanding that interact dynamically with one another."[26] According to Robbins, a text is a thick matrix of interwoven networks of meanings that extend far beyond the boundaries typically constructed that are used to analyze and interpret phenomena. A subset of the various textural components of sociorhetorical analysis that affects interpretation – intertexture – explores other texts in relation to aspects internal to the text being interpreted. It has been said that there is no greater commentary to the Scriptures than the Scriptures themselves; hence, an intertextual analysis has the potential for a greater degree of scriptural integrity in regards to interpretation. In his book entitled *An Introduction to the New Testament: Contexts, Methods & Ministry Formation*, David deSilva explained how New Testament authors oftentimes utilized quotes, alluded to events, echoed phrases, and reconfigured the pattern of familiar narratives from Old Testament and intertestamental literature or even borrowed from Greco–Roman and Hellenistic Jewish traditions that are written into the new texts that they create.[27] According to deSilva, intertexture occurs when "authors frequently weave the words of older, existing texts (whether those texts are written or passed on orally, ancient or contemporary) into the next text they create."[28] deSilva also explained how intertextural analysis provides a *window* into how an author shapes and interprets existing traditions in the process of presenting and forming situations. According to Robbins, *cultural intertexture* involves "symbolic worlds that particular communities of discourse nurture with special nuances and emphases."[29] Robbins explained that cultural intertexture appears in text in the form of *echoes* that occur when a word or phrase evokes a cultural tradition.

The echoes in 1 Thessalonians 2 verses 7-8 and 11-12 derive from the cultural traditions that were established early by Jesus Christ and passed on in the teachings of the apostles. According to Guy, Christianity first appeared to be a sect within Judaism; however, with Christianity and Judaism sharing common traditions and common Scriptures, the two faiths intersected and influenced each other. Eventually, Christianity would become a distinctive subculture within the Jewish culture of the first century. Guy explained that despite some ongoing interrelationships, the chasm between the Jewish and Christian communities became "increasingly deep and permanent."[30] Christianity would eventually become a culture in and of itself. It is this unique first-century Christian culture that influenced Paul and his writings.

The apostle Paul's selection of words in 1 Thessalonians 2 verses 7-8 and 11-12 demonstrate echoes from the Christian cultural traditions that were initially established by Jesus Christ and passed orally through the teachings of the apostles. Let's examine the cultural echoes that interplay the distinctively descriptive words chosen by Paul that further illustrate the parental metaphors of mother and father towards a greater understanding of his particular leadership approach. This understanding will provide us with valuable insights into five distinctive elements that contribute towards the development of a strategic small church leadership approach.

Thalpo (Care)

The first element of this strategic leadership approach is that of *care*. In 1 Thessalonians 2:7, the apostle Paul uses the Greek participle *thalpo* to illustrate the kind of motherly image he was depicting in his appeal to the small church in Thessalonica. The definition of the Greek participle *thalpo* means to warm, keep warm; to cherish with tender love, or to foster with tender care.[31] This word demonstrates an echo of the concept of "care" that was embodied and taught by Christ and His apostles that shaped the early Christian culture. How might this concept of "care" be embodied in the context of contemporary small church leadership today?

It has often been said that people don't care what you know until they know that you care. As pastors, we want people to care what we know because what we know are the truths of Scripture, and those truths are life-changing. But before people care to hear what we know (and want to teach them), they first want to know that we care about them.

Caring is about showing genuine concern for people. It involves being interested in what goes on in people's lives. It's about getting to know their name, their spouse and kids, what they do for a living, their hobbies and interests. It's also about getting to know what worries and concerns them. What are the current problems and challenges they are facing? What is preoccupying their thoughts? What is causing them to lose sleep at night? As pastors, these are the questions we need to find answers to.

Pastors always seem to have something to say. They want to be heard. But one of the biggest ways to demonstrate care is to empathetically listen to people. James 1:19 says, "...be quick to hear, slow to speak..." Too often as pastors, we are quick to speak and give our counsel, advice, guidance, and direction. We should show people we care by empathetically listening to them. We ought to give people our fully undivided attention by making an effort to hang on their every word instead of being preoccupied in our thoughts or even formulating a ready response to what they're telling us. It's about walking in their shoes and trying as best as we can to relate to their circumstance and predicament. We need to try and best understand them and the emotions they are feeling. This helps reassure them that we not only understand but also care.

Caring is about being there for others. As tempting as it is as pastors to want to give counsel, advice, guidance, and direction, oftentimes people just want us to be present for them. Oftentimes they are not looking for us to try and fix their problem or situation;

instead, they just want someone who will simply be there for them. They're looking for a hand to hold, arms that will embrace them, or a shoulder that they can lean or even cry on. Caring is about being totally present for people, especially when they need us the most.

The small church is uniquely positioned to ensure each member is cared for. The closeness and intimacy that is cultivated in small churches can cause people to easily get to know one another. Small church pastors should demonstrate care for each member of their congregation.

Metadidomi (Share)

The second element of this strategic leadership approach is that of *share*. In 1 Thessalonians 2:8, the apostle Paul uses the Greek participle *metadidomi* to further illustrate the kind of motherly image he was depicting in his appeal to the small church in Thessalonica. The definition of the Greek participle *metadidomi* means to impart.[32] This word demonstrates an echo of the concept of "share" that was embodied and taught by Christ and His apostles that shaped the early Christian culture. How might this concept of "share" be embodied in the context of contemporary small church leadership today?

When you open the door of your life to someone, you invite him or her into wonderful possibilities that will not only impact their life profoundly but yours as well. In a figurative sense, sharing is about inviting other people into your life. It's about having fun together. It's also about working hard together. It's about sharing good times and bad times. It's about laughing together and crying together. It's about sharing victories and failures, joys and pains, lessons and experiences. Sharing is a unique part of life and community.

Sharing is about communion and fellowship. It's about the life you live together in community. 1 John 1:3 says, "...that which we have seen and heard we proclaim also to you, so that you too may have fellowship with us; and indeed our fellowship is with the Father and with his Son Jesus Christ." In this verse, the Greek word for "fellowship" is *koinonia* which means "the share which one has in anything."[33] Sharing involves the times we spend in fellowship together as a church. Fellowship is one of the greatest strengths of the small church. The intimacy, strong and lasting relationships, and the close-knit bonds that are fostered and built are a result of the fellowship that is prevalent in small churches.

In a literal sense, sharing also includes extending the material things that you own for others to also have and use. In 1 Timothy 6:18 it says, "...to be generous and ready to share..." Sharing is also about helping others out financially when you can. Acts 2:44-45 says, "And all who believed were together and had all things in common. And they were selling their possessions and belongings and distributing the proceeds to all, as any had need." Here we see this concept of sharing material and financial resources to meet the needs of others in the church. Small church pastors should be keen to identify needs in the church and encourage members to pull together and contribute material and financial resources to meet those needs. Small churches could also pull together and contribute material and financial resources to reach out and help meet the needs of those outside of the church as well.

It is evident that everyone doesn't have the same amount when it comes to financial and material resources, but everyone has been given the same amount of time – 24 hours a day. No one gets any more, and no one gets any less. This is one resource that we all get an equal share of and is also one of the most precious and valuable resources that we own. Sharing one's time is one of the most generous gifts that anyone could ever give simply because it is a part of your life that you can never get back. Sharing your time with others is a profound gesture that is expressed through sacrifice.

Sharing also involves being open and honest with others. It's about being vulnerable and sharing the thoughts of your heart. People value authenticity - what you see is what you get. Authenticity is about being real – real open and honest. Authenticity is another strength of the small church that lends well to genuine, strong, lasting and meaningful relationships.

The concept of sharing unites members in small churches in greater relational community. The sharing of our resources is a valuable investment in the life of others that yields extravagant returns and eternal rewards. Small church pastors should model the generosity of the concept of sharing.

Parakaleo (Exhort)

The third element of this strategic leadership approach is that of *exhort*. In 1 Thessalonians 2:12, the apostle Paul uses the Greek participle *parakaleo* to illustrate the kind of fatherly image he was depicting in his appeal to the small church in Thessalonica. The definition of the Greek participle *parakaleo* means to call to one's side, call for, summon; to address, speak to (call to, call upon), which may be done in the way of exhortation, entreaty, comfort, instruction, etc.; to admonish, exhort; to beg, entreat, beseech, to strive to appease by entreaty; to console, to encourage and strengthen by consolation, to comfort, to receive consolation, be comforted; to encourage, strengthen; exhorting and comforting and encouraging; and to instruct, teach.[34] This word demonstrates an echo of the concept of "exhort" that was embodied and taught by Christ and His apostles that shaped the early Christian culture. How might this concept of "exhort" be embodied in the context of contemporary small church leadership today?

Colossians 3:16 says, "Let the word of Christ dwell in you richly, teaching and admonishing one another in all wisdom…" Exhorting involves not just teaching but also admonishing. It is important for small church pastors to integrate both teaching and admonishing through the proper handling of God's Word in wisdom, discernment and sensitivity of the Holy Spirit's leading.

Exhorting also involves teaching and instructing by the sharing of knowledge. As I mentioned earlier, people don't care what you know until they know that you care. Pastors possess a wealth of biblical knowledge and spiritual experience. Small church pastors should be willing and eager to share that knowledge and experience to help others navigate the challenges of life by faith in Christ. But before people are willing to hear what we have to say and offer, they first need to know that we love and care for them. Therefore, exhorting should not just merely be teaching and instructing; neither should it simply be counseling, advising, admonishing, or warning. It should be all of these things encapsulated in the love, care, and concern for those we undershepherd as pastors and walk with as brothers and sisters in Christ.

As small church pastors, we have been afforded wonderful opportunities to exhort God's people. Whether it be in the capacity of preaching over the pulpit, or teaching or facilitating a Bible study, or counseling in an office, or praying for someone, or even in casual conversation and dialog, we should faithfully minister the truth of God's Word wrapped and seasoned with God's love and grace for His people. It should never be ministered coldly or matter-of-factly, but in a manner that causes others to be built up in the Lord. 1 Corinthians 8:1 says, '...we know that "all of us possess knowledge." This "knowledge" puffs up, but love builds up.' When we exhort others by providing instruction, counsel or guidance, our intention should be for the building up of people and not tearing down – for encouraging and not discouraging.

Admonishing and warning is also an essential aspect of the concept of exhorting. It is during these opportunities that we should be careful as to how we minister God's Word and counsel. It should be done prayerfully, sensitively, and filled with grace and love. Administered in this fashion, exhorting through admonition will be received by others with the presupposition that it was done with genuine love, care, and concern with their best interests in mind.

Exhorting is about speaking into someone's life. But you have to earn the right to speak into someone's life, especially when you have to say the difficult things in love. When you demonstrate genuine love and concern for the people you lead as their pastor, they will give you permission to speak into their lives and receive what you have to say.

When God's Word is the central focus of the church, and is freely ministered through exhortation, then healing, redemption, and health will prevail (Ps 107:20). Hebrews 4:12 illustrates how powerful and life-changing God's Word is. So allow the truth and power of God's Word to render its work in the life of God's church by teaching, instructing, counseling, advising, and admonishing in love and grace.

Paramytheomai (Encourage)

The fourth element of this strategic leadership approach is that of *encourage*. In 1 Thessalonians 2:12, the apostle Paul uses the Greek participle *paramytheomai* to further illustrate the kind of fatherly image he was depicting in his appeal to the small church in Thessalonica. The definition of Greek participle *paramytheomai* means to speak to, address one, whether by way of admonition and incentive, or to calm and console; to encourage.[35] This word demonstrates an echo of the concept of "encourage" that was embodied and taught by Christ and His apostles that shaped the early Christian culture. How might this concept of "encourage" be embodied in the context of contemporary small church leadership today?

I recently found a quote circulating around the Internet with an unknown author that says, "Encouragement is like oxygen to the human spirit. Don't forget you're carrying someone's air. Encourage them; help them breathe." This is so true. For the Christian, we have a bountiful supply of encouragement from God's Word. The Bible is filled with the life giving words of God; it is the very breath of God (1 Timothy 3:16). As Christians, we can share the words that have tremendous potential to strengthen the heart and uplift the soul. 1 Thessalonians 5:11 says, "...encourage one another and build each other up..." Encouraging is about inspiring courage and confidence in people. Encouragement strengthens and empowers people to rise to new heights that they can only dream of. Small church pastors serve not only as coaches but also as cheerleaders; they not only give direction and guidance but support and encouragement.

There is tremendous latent potential that is stored up in every Christian that is ready to be unleashed in good works. God has great and wonderful plans in store for each of us as we walk by faith and trust Him in humble obedience. Ephesians 2:10 tells us, "For we are his workmanship, created in Christ Jesus for good works, which God prepared beforehand, that we should walk in them." Jesus said in John 14:12, "Truly, truly, I say to you, whoever believes in me will also do the works that I do; and greater works than these will he do, because I am going to the Father." Sometimes we just need that little bit of encouragement to step out confidently and courageously and accomplish all of the wonderfully great and glorious things that God has ordained for us. Encouragement fuels God's people to step out in faith and accomplish these great works for the glory of God.

Encouraging also comes in the form of comforting and consoling others. In John 16:33, Jesus said, "In the world you will have tribulation." It is inevitable that people will face difficult times in their lives, and it is during these times when they will desperately need encouragement to keep them moving forward. Small church pastors should encourage others by strengthening their resolve in the midst of the challenges and difficulties they face. Encouragement can also be a valuable outreach tool for the small church. The close-knit relationships, that are a source of encouragement for members of small churches, should actively and purposefully extend to those outside of the church as well.

Encouragement comes also in a variety of forms and gestures. Sometimes encouragement can come in words and other times with no words at all. As heartfelt and good-natured your words and counsel may be, it could be given only to fall on deaf ears. It is therefore essential to discern when to say something and when not to. Sometimes just your silent presence will mean a great deal of encouragement. Encouragement might come in the form of a prayer, a hug, or a helping hand. It can even come in the form of a gift or service. Encouragement can also come in the form of an invitation – an invitation to lunch, coffee, or to church. Encouragement is a gift that cost very little to give but is of immense value for those on the receiving end.

Small church pastors should constantly encourage people towards faith and trust in God. Small churches should be a flowing source of encouragement for those who are in desperation, discouragement, and hopelessness. Small church pastors should foster a culture and environment of encouragement through the intimate and close-knit family-like relationships prevalent in small churches. This kind of an environment should flourish and be an overflowing source for all in need.

Martyreo (Charge)

The fifth element of this strategic leadership approach is that of *charge*. In 1 Thessalonians 2:12, the apostle Paul used the Greek participle *martyreo* to also further illustrate the kind of fatherly image he was depicting in his appeal to the small church in Thessalonica. The definition of the Greek participle *martyreo* means to be a witness, to bear witness, to affirm that one has been seen or heard or experienced something, or that he knows it because taught by divine revelation or inspiration; to give (not to keep back) testimony; to utter honorable testimony, give a good report; and conjure, implore.[36] This word demonstrates an echo of the concept of "charge" that was embodied and taught by Christ and His apostles that shaped the early Christian culture. How might this concept of "charge" be embodied in the context of contemporary small church leadership today?

To be inspired is energizing, but to inspire someone is catapulting. Charging is about challenging, urging, motivating, and inspiring others towards great things in God. People have inner yearnings to be a part of or to accomplish something meaningful and significant. Charging is about awakening God-given dreams within the hearts of people that propel them into action causing these dreams to become reality.

God's Word is filled with commands that are designed to engage our faith in ways that produce fruitful manifestations of the kingdom of heaven within us and around us. They are divine commands that call God's people to a greater love for and obedience to God. God's Word is filled with inspiration. It challenges us to become better for God, for ourselves, and for others. It calls us to a greater, bigger, more profound and meaningful purpose in life.

Charge is about being commissioned. Discipleship is all about answering the charge – the charge of the Great Commission. Matthew 28:19 charges us to "go and make disciples." The charge of the Great Commission includes the component to teach others to obey God. Obedience is another component of this charge and is the greatest reflection of a growing love for God. Jesus said in John 14:15, "If you love me, you will keep my commandments." Discipleship is entering into a committed, devoted and growing relationship with Jesus that is expressed in a growing love for Him and others. It is the fulfillment of the

Great Commission that prompts the Great Commandment to love God with all of our heart, mind, soul, and strength and to love one another. There is nothing more meaningful and significant than the Great Commission and the Great Commandment as the greatest inner yearnings inherent within every redeemed soul. Charging is a matter of awakening and inspiring these inherent yearnings in others.

Hebrews 10:24 says, "And let us consider how to stir up one another to love and good works." Exhorting is about stirring up others to love that is expressed in good deeds of service to one another. Of all the charges contained in the Scriptures, love is the greatest. 1 Corinthians 13:13 says, "So now faith, hope, and love abide, these three; but the greatest of these is love." The greatest charge is to love. From love comes an outpouring of good deeds. 1 Corinthians 3:9 says, "For we are God's fellow workers..." As Christians, we have the great honor and privilege to be partners with God in the advancing of His kingdom here on earth through the work God has charged us to do. It is the role of the small church pastor to charge or stir up others towards obedience to God towards the working of these "good deeds" for God's greater redemptive purposes in the world.

Small church pastors should motivate and inspire their members towards faithful obedience to God's Word and purposes. Small church pastors help God's people see the grandeur vision of God's purposes. Small church pastors inspire others towards obedience to God in the accomplishment of this grandeur vision. It is the kind of vision and purpose that extend far beyond our lives and ourselves.

The possibilities of God's redemptive work are endless when people are elevated to higher places of faith in Christ. Motivating and inspiring people to see beyond their selfish ambitions and idiosyncratic views to God's greater work and purpose positions them to take on the charge of their holy callings.

CHAPTER 14
Conclusion (Section 2)

Two talents leadership is about small church leadership. It's about faithfully serving the small church. I personally believe that the concept of the "two talents leadership" approach is a focus on the New Testament pastoral ministry model. The Greek word used for pastor in the New Testament is *poimen* which literally means shepherd.[37] With an understanding that Jesus Christ is the Great and Good Shepherd (John 10:11), we as pastors are considered His undershepherds. Jesus instructed Peter in John 21:15 to "Feed my lambs" and in verse 16 to "Tend my sheep." Peter in turn instructed pastors in 1 Peter 5:2-3 to "...shepherd the flock of God that is among you, exercising oversight, not under compulsion, but willingly, as God would have you; not for shameful gain, but eagerly; not domineering over those in your charge, but being examples to the flock." The New Testament pastoral ministry model focuses on people – on shepherding and discipling people. Pastoring has always been all about people.

In a culture where the notion of bigger is oftentimes mistakenly considered better, small church pastors are relentlessly and painstakingly trying to grow their churches. This is not a bad thing, but the obsession to do so is. In the process, small church pastors have taken on leadership paradigms that are unsuitable to their unique ministry context. In an attempt to become larger churches, small church pastors have adopted more contemporary forms of larger church leadership models and structures from resources that originated from the church growth movement. In doing so, they have become more like executive administrators. They focus on managing programs, structures, systems, budgets and facilities. They focus on hiring and maintaining staff as well as coordinating volunteers. They have become preoccupied with the "workings" of church rather than the church itself - the people. They no longer operate as pastors in the *poimen* sense of the word but rather as organizational executives and administrators. For larger churches, this is not a bad thing. It becomes practically essential for larger churches to operate in such a manner in order to function and even survive. When you have that many people that God has placed you charge over, managing elaborate and oftentimes complex systems and ministry structures are necessary. But when you're a small church, similar systems and ministry structures are not necessarily required but rather can actually become complications and obstructions to the work of ministry that is unique for small churches. It is tempting for small churches to try and want to grow numerically by overextending themselves in both ministry as well as in their leadership approach. As I mention in my first book *Don't Supersize It! 10 Healthy Perspectives of the Small Church*, "When you discover your unique strengths as a small church in your particular context of ministry, it will empower you to not only stay focused but also prevent you from overextending yourself."[38] By being preoccupied with the "workings" of the church, many small church pastors are treating their small churches more like businesses rather than like families.

Strategic small church leadership development hinges on small churches capitalizing on their inherent strengths. The small church would gain in optimizing its leadership approach by realizing and considering its family dimensional strength. With one of its primary strengths being its family dimension, the small church can capitalize on the development of a unique and dynamic leadership approach by juxtaposing a leadership structure that is congruent with that of a family. In his book entitled *Church 3.0: Upgrades for the Future Church*, author Neil Cole argued that church is no longer an event to be at but a family of which to be a part.[39] The intimate family dimensional strength of the small church lends towards a biblical leadership approach that focuses and adopts biblical values and traits inherent in the roles of spiritual fathers and mothers - this is what makes this leadership approach strategic. The leadership values and traits espoused by the apostle Paul in 1 Thessalonians 2 verses 7-8 and 11-12 provide a framework for the development and employment of a strategic small church leadership approach.

At the writing of this book, I have currently thirty-nine souls that attend the small church I pastor. Each one of them means a great deal to me because God found it in His grace to allow me to be their pastor. I frequently meet with my associate pastor to discuss ministry. At one of our most recent meetings, I told my associate pastor that when I think of ministry, I don't think of programs, strategies, plans, structures, finances, etc. I told him that what I do think about when it comes to ministry is people – each an every individual soul that attends our church. I think of all the various aspects of each of their lives and their challenges, and I think of how I can encourage and inspire them to walk by faith and love God more and more. For me, pastoring is all about the people of God. I was called to pastor people and not administer and manage programs, structures, plans or finances. For me, pastoring is about loving people by caring for them, sharing my life with them, teaching and encouraging them in God's Word, and inspiring them towards God's amazing and incredible plan for their lives. So if you ask me the reasons why this strategic leadership approach for the small church is so important, right now I can personally give you thirty-nine really good ones!

ENDNOTES
Section 2

1. Bob DeSagun, *Don't Supersize It! 10 Healthy Perspectives for the Small Church* (San Bernardino, CA: CreateSpace, 2015), 18.
2. David Livermore, *Leading With Cultural Intelligence: The Real Secret To Success* (New York, NY: AMACOM, 2015), ix.
3. Gill Robinson Hickman, *Leading Organizations: Perspectives For A New Era (2nd Edition)* (Los Angeles, CA: SAGE Publications, 2010), 3.
4. DeSagun, 34.
5. Ibid, 36.
6. Ibid, 38.
7. Ibid, 40.
8. Brandon J. O'Brien, *The Strategically Small Church* (Minneapolis, MN: Bethany House Publishers, 2010), 30.
9. Laurie Guy, *Introducing Early Christianity: A Topical Survey of Its Life, Belief & Practices* (Downers Grove, IL: InterVarsity Press, 2004), 23.
10. Ibid, 24.
11. R. Kevin Seasoltz, "Sacred Space, The Arts and Theology: Some Light From History" (*Worship*, *82*(6), 2008), 519-542.
12. Tom Sine, *The New Conspirators: Creating The Future One Mustard Seed At A Time* (Downers Grove, IL: InterVarsity Press, 2008), 257.
13. Brian Hearne, "Christian Family Life: Some Pastoral Priorities" (*AFER*, *24*(5), 1982), 290.

14. O'Brien, 133.
15. Ibid, 126.
16. Ibid, 137.
17. Tony Dale, Felcity Dale & George Barna, *Small Is Big: Unleashing the Big Impact of Intentionally Small Churches* (Carol Stream, IL: Tyndale House Publishers, 2011), 46.
18. Livermore, 87.
19. Timothy Laniak, *Shepherds After My Own Heart: Pastoral Traditions and Leadership in the Bible* (Downers Grove, IL: InterVarsity Press, 2006), 35.
20. Ibid, 39.
21. Andrew Clarke, *A Pauline Theology of Church Leadership* (New York, NY: Bloomsbury Publishing, 2008), 137.
22. Andrew Clarke, *Serve the Community of the Church: Chrisitans As Leaders and Ministers* (Grand Rapids, MI: William B. Eerdmans Publishing Company, 2000), 162.
23. Jeffrey Weima, "Infants, Nursing Mother, and Father: Paul's Portrayal of a Pastor" (*Calvin Theological Journal, 37*(2), 2002), 209-229.
24. Ibid.
25. Dermot Power, *A Spiritual Theology of the Priesthood: The Mystery of Christ and the Mission of the Priest.* (Washington, DC: The Catholic University of America Press, 1998).
26. Vernon Robbins, *The Tapestry of Early Christian Discourse: Rhetoric, Society, and Ideology* (New York, NY: Routledge, 1996), 22.
27. David deSilva, *An Introduction to the New Testament: Contexts, Methods & Ministry*

Formation (Downers Grove, IL: InterVarsity Press).

28. Ibid, 800.
29. Robbins, 115.
30. Guy, 14.
31. Adapted from http://www.blueletterbible.org/lang/lexicon/lexicon.cfm?Strongs=G2282&t=KJV
32. Adapted from http://www.blueletterbible.org/lang/lexicon/lexicon.cfm?Strongs=G3330&t=KJV
33. Adapted from http://www.blueletterbible.org/lang/lexicon/lexicon.cfm?Strongs=G2842&t=KJV
34. Adapted from http://www.blueletterbible.org/lang/lexicon/lexicon.cfm?Strongs=G3870&t=KJV
35. Adapted from http://www.blueletterbible.org/lang/lexicon/lexicon.cfm?Strongs=G3888&t=KJV
36. Adapted from http://www.blueletterbible.org/lang/lexicon/lexicon.cfm?Strongs=G3140&t=KJV
37. Adapted from http://www.blueletterbible.org/lang/lexicon/lexicon.cfm?Strongs=G4166&t=KJV
38. DeSagun, 61-62.
39. Neil Cole, *Church 3.0: Upgrades for the Future Church* (San Francisco, CA: Jossey-Bass, 2010).

SECTION 3
HEALTH

From the book
GARDENING MADE SIMPLE
Cultivating Healthy Ministry
In The Small Church

Recently the topic of church growth has been rightly replaced with that of church health. In the past, the health of a church has been overly and obsessively predicated by its size. But a church can be either healthy or unhealthy despite its size. Bob DeSagun has been encouraging and inspiring small churches to look past their attendance numbers and deeper to much more meaningful aspects of their small church ministry. But how can small churches ensure that they are considered healthy despite their size? In this book, Bob DeSagun provides the small church with some valuable insights, ministry practices, and his personal list of "metrics" that are designed to help cultivate health in the small church.

CHAPTER 15
Introduction (Section 3)

My first two books on the small church were designed to encourage small churches and their pastors who struggle with feelings of insecurity, insignificance, and failure because of the size of their churches. My first book *Don't Supersize It! 10 Healthy Perspectives for the Small Church* provides 10 healthy perspectives designed to encourage small churches.[1] My second book *Two Talents Leadership: A Strategic Small Church Leadership Approach* provides small church pastors will a healthy leadership approach.[2] My aim in both of these books was not only to encourage my readers but inspire them in leading and serving in their small churches. The insights that I provide in these books were from a compilation of information and research I gained from my doctoral studies along with many years of experience pastoring and serving a small church. I developed healthy perspectives for ministry and found relief from all the pressure of thinking that I had to grow the church I was pastoring into some huge megachurch. I finally was able to accept that I was fine as a pastor and so was my small church. We were good. We were healthy. But were we?

It wasn't until a recent meeting that I had with my district superintendent did I start to entertain this question of whether or not we were healthy. During the meeting I had with my district superintendent, he challenged me in regards to some of the concepts and principles that I as asserting in my books. It wasn't that he disagreed with any of the concepts or principle, but he couldn't help but express a concern he had that caused a "yellow flag" of caution to be raised for him personally. His concerned was that though the concepts and principles in my books were both true and encouraging for the small church, they could also inadvertently give unhealthy small churches an excuse to remain where they are and fail to do the things that they should be doing to move towards health. I was in complete agreement with him. Just because a small church is small, doesn't necessarily make it an unhealthy church. But in the same argument, it does make it necessarily a healthy one either.

Recently the topic of church growth has been rightly replaced with that of church health. In the past, the health of the church has been overly and obsessively predicated by its size. In other words, if a church was big, then it must be healthy; and if a church was small, then it must be unhealthy. Small churches have been unjustly summed up on this sole parameter and have more than often received the short end of the stick. The truth to the matter is a church can either be healthy or unhealthy despite its size. Fortunately a new surge of literature has begun to trickle into the Christian market advocating for newer and more substantially meaningful "metrics" for church health. The determination of the health of a church has slowly moved away from numbers and on to better and much more significant and meaningful measures – many of which still cannot be measured numerically.

This book is designed to provide you and your small church with some insights, guidance, and encouragement towards cultivating healthy ministry practices that perpetuate Great Commission fulfillment. Jesus used horticultural and agricultural analogies to illustrate timeless divine truths regarding the kingdom of God. He talked about sowing seeds (Mark 4:3), putting your hand to the plow (Luke 9:62), pruning (John 15:2), He even talked about fruits (Matt 7:17), flowers (Luke 12:27) and even weeds (Matt 13:26). I will make an attempt in this book to do the same by using the term "gardening" as an analogy to the work that still needs to be accomplished in the whole scheme of discipleship and Great Commission fulfillment towards healthy small church ministry. In the past few years, the word "simple" has been used in ecclesiology to describe a movement characterized by smaller more organic churches. Simple is about small churches engaging in biblically natural forms of ministry that stem from practices found in the early New Testament church. *Gardening Made Simple* is about ministry practices that help to promote healthy small churches.

CHAPTER 16
The Variables

Part of my doctoral study involved conducting social science research. One important aspect of research is understanding how the different variables involved affect the results of the research. There are some variables that the researcher will be able to control and then there are others that they will be unable to control. Just as in social science research, there are variables in ministry that you will be able to control and others that you will not. It is important to understand the variables involved and which ones you can and cannot control.

We all want to feel like we are in control. Everybody has control issues to some degree. We want control, for the most part, to ensure that things turn out the way we want them to. We want to control aspects of our jobs, our relationships, our finances, our families, and our kids. We have our idea of how life's situations should turn out or at least how we want them to turn out, and we want control of those outcomes.

We feel safe and secure when things are under control. We feel safe and secure when we have things under our control. We all want to feel safe, and we all want to feel secure. We feel safe and secure when we can control the fact that the front door is locked at night, or that we are fully covered on our insurance policy, or when we have a sound financial portfolio in place for retirement. When we are in control of the outcome, then we feel a sense of safety and security.

We feel successful when things are under control. We feel successful when we have things under our control. We feel successful when we can control the outcome of things and have them turn out the way we want or the way we imagine. When we know that the calculations we make will yield a particular outcome, then we feel a sense of achievement and success. When our homes are locked and our families are safe throughout the evening, we feel successful. When our insurance policy covers the damage to our homes or vehicles, or if the medical insurance covers the cost of the hospital bills, we feel that we've done our job preparing and that gives us a sense of success. When our financial portfolios yield a good investment and that we are able to retire early or on time without any financial worries, we feel that we've achieved success. Control gives us a sense of success.

Understanding what you are able to control is paramount when cultivating a healthy small church atmosphere and environment. When God calls you to a particular aspect of small church ministry, He will also give you complete power, authority, and control over those variables of ministry. When God created and called Adam, He gave him command over the earth (Gen 1:28). Jesus called His disciples and gave them authority to perform certain ministries (Matt 10:1). Understand that God will call you as a small church

128

leader to do a particular aspect of ministry and will give you not only complete power, authority, and resources to fulfill it but also full control over it. Here is the big truth though – that aspect of ministry is not the growth of your church! Surprise! Too often we think, as pastors, that church growth is our responsibility. That is an unbiblical precedence and has been the biggest frustration of small church pastors.

It is unbiblical to say that church growth is the role or responsibility of the church or of its pastors. The concept of church growth stemmed from a mid-twentieth century human conception that eventually proliferated and eventually morphed into an ecclesiological construct disguised with an ennobling yet unbiblical premise. If we take a closer look at the Holy Scriptures, we find that Acts 2:47 tells us that the Lord added to their numbers; 1 Corinthians 3:6 tells us that God will provide the growth; and in Matthew 16:18, Jesus said that He will build His church. These foundational verses explain that it is God who has the primary role and responsibility to grow His church. Now that does not negate the role and responsibility that each member of the body of Christ is called to play (we'll get more into this in next couple of chapters).

Growth is not the responsibility of the church and therefore should not be its focus. Our focus should be on the control variables – the variables or aspects of ministry that God has given us power, authority, and control over. Not only has God given us control over these variables but, according to 1 Corinthians 3:13, He is also holding us responsible for them. But church growth is not one of them, and yet it is this one variable that continues to hampered many small church pastors and leaders.

The first significant aspect to recognize and understand are the variables that we, as small church pastors and leaders, are able control and distinguish them from those that we cannot. Trying to control variables in ministry that were not designed for us nor our church to control will only frustrate us. Focusing on the variables that we are able to control will allow us to become effective and productive in ministry. This concept of control is similar to the serenity prayer:

> *God, grant me the serenity to accept*
> *the things I cannot change,*
> *The courage to change the things I can,*
> *And the wisdom to know the difference.*

There will be some aspects of ministry that you will not be able to change, and there will be aspect of ministry that you will be able to. The things we cannot change, we have no control over; but the things that we can change, we have either complete or at least some degree of control over. Understanding and discerning the difference between variables in ministry that we can control and those that we cannot can be the most liberating and most empowering moment in your ministry. Focus on the variables that you can control and leave the rest to God.

CHAPTER 17
The Task

Understanding that it is God's role and responsibility to grow His church is one thing, understanding that we as Christians have an entirely different role and responsibility is another. This is the part of the book where I begin to address the concern that my district superintendent had regarding some of the assertions in my previous books regarding the small church. What is our responsibility in ministry? This can best be seen in 1 Corinthians 3:5-15:

> [5]What, after all, is Apollos? And what is Paul? Only servants, through whom you came to believe – as the Lord assigned to each his task. [6]I planted the seed, Apollos watered it, but God has been making it grow. [7]So neither the one who plants nor the one who waters is anything, but only God, who makes things grow. [8]The one who plants and the one who waters have one purpose, and they will each be rewarded according to their own labor. [9]For we are co-workers in God's service; you are God's field, God's building.
>
> [10]By the grace God has given me, I laid a foundation as a wise builder, and someone else is building on it. But each one should build with care. [11]For no one can lay any foundation other than the one already laid, which is Jesus Christ. [12]If anyone builds on this foundation using gold, sliver, costly stones, wood, hay or straw, [13]their work will be shown for what it is, because the Day will bring it to light. It will be revealed with fire, and the fire will test the quality of each person's work. [14]If what has been built survives, the builder will receive a reward. [15]If it is burned up, the builder will suffer loss but yet will be

saved – even though only as one escaping through the flames.

In this passage, the apostle Paul was addressing factions regarding loyalty to a preferred teacher (in this particular case it was either to Paul or to Apollos) that only demonstrated the spiritual immaturity of the believers in Corinth. Aside from this, there is much that we can learn as a small church from this passage. Verse 5 tells us that the Lord assigns each of us a task in this great ongoing redemptive work to cause His kingdom to come here on earth as it is in heaven. Each of us as Christians play a vital role in this work, and it is important for us to discover this role in Christ. Verse 6 tells us that God is ultimately responsible for the growth and expansion of His church. Though it is God's role to grow His church, we each have been given a role as well whether it be "planting" or "watering." Planting may refer to the initial presentation of the gospel message whereas watering may refer to the building up and maturing of the believer's faith in Christ. Verse 8 tells us that both "planting" and "watering" are individual roles that collectively fulfill God's ordained purpose in the bringing about of His kingdom here on earth. Verse 9 tells us that we are "co-workers" together with God in fulfilling His ordained purpose to bring about His kingdom. This is the great honor and privilege that God has granted each of us in assigning unto us the task of planting or watering. That is why verse 10 tells us that it is by God's grace are we able to participate in His great work of bringing about His kingdom. The remaining verses of this passage explain how the privileged work we do will be tested in the end on the day of glory. The work that we have done in our own strength and power will not stand, but the work we do by God's grace as we yield and work obediently alongside and in the power of the Holy Spirit will stand and last for all eternity. This is why we should always give ourselves fully to the work of the Lord because we do not want our labor to be in vain (1 Cor 15:58).

In the whole scheme of things, the primary point that I want for us to see from this passage is that there is a definitive work that God does, and there is also a definitive work that we do as well. As small churches, we don't just stand by and think (after reading my first book) that we're fine and that there's nothing further we need do. If that's what you got out of my first book, then you miss my point entirely. No, there is still so much work ahead of us. It is a work that is not only honorable and privileged but also necessary. It is a great honor have been extended such a divine invitation to be a part of it all that brings meaning and purpose to our lives.

Paul phrases this divine work in agricultural terms (much like Christ did in His ministry) – by using the terms planting and watering. Oftentimes as small churches we are so focused on wanting to grow our churches unbeknownst that it is God's part and not ours. Our part is to plant. Our part is to water. As I mentioned earlier, Paul may have referred to planting as the initial presentation of the gospel message whereas watering may have referred to the subsequent work of building up and maturing the believer's faith in Christ. Regardless of the distinction, the work is indicative of the mandate we, as followers of Jesus, are all called to fulfill – the Great Commission. The Great Commission calls us to go and make disciples of all nations, baptizing them in the name of the Father and of the Son and of the Holy Spirit, and teaching them to obey everything that Jesus has commanded us (Matt 28:19). In essence, the task of planting and watering is all about making disciples. It is about proclaiming the gospel message, inviting lost people into a loving and personal relationship with Jesus Christ as their Lord and Savior, and building them up and maturing them in their faith in Christ so that they in turn can do the same for others who are lost. What that looks like for each of us in our own unique small church ministry context we'll discuss in the next chapter. But the fact of the matter is, there is still much work to be done. Jesus said, "The harvest is plentiful but the workers are few. Ask the Lord of the harvest, therefore, to send out workers into his harvest field" (Matt 9:37-38). There is still much work that needs to be done, and the small church is still part of God's plan to complete that work. God's task is to grow His church, and our task is to obey and rely upon the Holy Spirit as we partner with Him in the discipleship of ourselves and others towards fulfilling the Great Commission.

CHAPTER 18
The Context

Context is one of the most important facets of ministry work because it not only defines the kind of work but also predetermines the parameters of that work. As Christians, we all have a part to play in the task that God has assigned to us in the going and making of disciples. The task of discipleship is fairly broad, but your context of ministry will determine how that is going to look like in a regular day-to-day practice. But how do we discover that context? How do we discover what the Lord is calling our small church to do and how to do it?

We get our vision and mission from God; it is not something we create ourselves. God gives us direction and guidance for our lives and ministries. He has a plan and purpose for every single member of the body of Christ. God also has a plan and purpose for every single local church – to include your small church. We see in 1 Corinthians 12 that each member of the body of Christ has a specific and unique role to play, and each local church has a specific and unique role to play as well. We don't create that for ourselves. We have to clearly and distinctly hear God's call for our own personal lives as well as for our small churches. Whatever the task is that God will call us to, we can clearly discern it only if we are in tune with the Holy Spirit. No two ministry contexts will be exactly alike; therefore, it is important to stop trying to replicate successful practices and models from one ministry context and assume that it will be successful in another (particularly your own). The model, method and approach for your particular and unique small church ministry context have already been predetermined by God. Therefore it is imperative that you, as a small church pastor or leader, seek after the Lord and hear directly from Him. I think too often we have sought out and consulted with various supposed experts in the ministry field, popular Christian resource literature, celebrity Christian pastors and personalities and their teachings, and the latest ministry fads and trends; yet we have failed to seek out the one true source - God. I am not saying that any of these things I mentioned are bad or unreliable; but if they are used, they should only confirm what God has already revealed to you as a result of seeking after Him first. The parameters of your specific and unique ministry context have already been predetermined by God; therefore, it is imperative that we seek Him in prayer so that He may reveal this to us personally.

Throughout the gospel accounts we see the practice and lifestyle of prayer modeled in the life and ministry of Jesus Christ. Jesus understood the importance of His connection through prayer to the Father not only as a mode of communication but also as a window that allowed Him to see into the heavens from whence the Father did His work. Jesus said,

"Very truly I tell you, the Son can do nothing by himself; he can do only what he sees his Fathering doing, because whatever the Father does the Son also does. For the Father loves the Son and shows him all he does. Yes, and he will show him even greater works than these, so that you will be amazed" (John 5:19-20). Jesus sought after His Father in prayer so that He would not only stay in sync with Him but also receive His marching orders. Jesus was constantly seeking after His Father in prayer (Luke 5:16). Jesus was so in tune with the Father that He only did what He saw the Father doing. Prayer keeps us constantly connected to the Father's direction every step of the way. Jesus said, "I seek not to please myself but him who sent me" (John 5:30). Prayer was also a way that Jesus kept Himself centered in on His Father's will as opposed to His own. Even in His darkest hour in the Garden of Gethsemane did Jesus pray, "Father, if you are willing, take this cup from me; yet not my will, but yours be done" (Luke 22:42). Prayer helps keep us from seeking our own will and plans for our small churches and keeps us centered on seeking after God's will and plan instead. Jesus clearly understood the necessity of prayer and so should we.

We need to be so in tune with God that we do not exert efforts anywhere else other than where God is calling us in ministry. Our first step is to seek the Father's will through prayer. Small church pastors and leaders need to walk so closely to God so that they are aware of the Father's call, leading and direction for their ministries. It is vital that we as small church pastors and leaders seek the Father in constant prayer as to our unique and distinct marching orders for our individual ministry contexts. The first place to discover and discern the context of our ministries as well as the intricate details of the work God is calling each of us as small church pastors and leaders is in prayer. Prayer will not only provide us God's direction for our contextual ministry but also conviction and clarity in regards to employing and executing His plan. As we seek the Lord in prayer, He will reveal to us His plans for our distinct and unique ministry context. The context that He will reveal to us will provide the parameters for our small church ministry. Our ministry context will allow us to discern what God has called us to do, where God has called us to do it, with whom God will call us to do it with, when God will call us to do it, and how God will call us to do it. It will also help us to discern what God is not calling us to do as well. Knowing exactly what God has called us to do will assist us in faithfully stewarding the resources that He will provided for us to fulfill that calling. But all of this will not come but by prayer.

There is no bypassing this critical process or taking any kind of shortcut, for prayer is paramount for not only seeking God's will and direction for our small churches but for the impact that our ministries will make for eternity. The character of our ministry will also be determined by the character of our prayer life. The amount of time we spend in prayer connecting with God will be reflected in the quality, depth and impact of our ministries. One of the core values of the denomination for which I belong to is that "prayer is the primary work of God's people."[3] When we pray, something incredibly powerful, supernaturally mysterious, yet supremely divine is set into motion in our lives, in the lives of others, and in the world around us that causes God's good plan to be executed with the precision of His divine hand and not our own. Prayer is not a precursor to the work; it is the work. Prayer supersedes all other work in ministry. The details of our specific and unique ministry context has already been predetermined by God; therefore, it is imperative that we seek Him in prayer so that He may reveal this to us personally.

CHAPTER 19
The Faithful

It was a dream come true when me and my wife bought our very first house. It was a small two-story, three bedroom, two-and-a-half bath, detached home. It was only a couple of years old, which meant that the small backyard that came with it was already landscaped. To our surprise, the previous owners had created an incredibly beautiful lavish garden with various plants, bushes, and flowers. There was a small patch of grass that surrounded a beautiful stone pathway. After our purchase, I made a few additions to the garden to include some smooth stone décor, a makeshift firepot, and a couple of wooden lawn chairs to add some quaintness and serenity to the garden scene. Every late afternoon, I was out there in the garden doing some light pruning and watering. I considered that time every day as a wonderful opportunity to reflect, pray and simply wind down from the day's activity as I got out there in the backyard to tend and water the garden. For the first few months, I was faithful to get out there and "do my thing." It was actually a time that I looked forward to every day. After some time, for whatever reasons, I began to neglect the garden out back. In just a few months, that quaint little lush garden became a horrid jungle of overgrown shrubs and weeds. One day my father-in-law came over to visit and noticed the jungle out back and pressured me to get out there and cut everything down (with his help). In a couple of hours, the once lavish garden was now a dry and barren desert of a space. My lack of faithfulness caused a thing of beauty to become one of ashes. I'm reminded of the Fall when Adam's sin caused God to curse the ground and turn the lavish Garden of Eden into a land that yielded thorns and thistles (Gen 3:17-18).

Throughout the Bible, unfaithfulness has been a prominent characteristic theme of man's response and relationship to God. Story after story in the Bible do we see how prominent biblical characters demonstrated an unfaithfulness to God - starting with the first man Adam in his sin of disobedience that was the reason for the Fall, the Israelites idolatry and complaining in the desert of Sinai, king David's abuse of his position to take Bathsheba for himself, the evil kings throughout Israel's history that led them into captivity and exile, and Peter's denial and Judas' betrayal of Jesus. Instance after instance of man's unfaithfulness to God is displayed throughout the pages of Scripture. Yet despite our unfaithfulness, God continues to remain faithful (2 Tim 2:13).

In my second book, I coined the term "Two Talents Leadership" to describe a ministry leadership context that juxtaposes God's divine providence with a servant leader's faithful stewardship - it describes how a servant leader faithfully stewards a smaller measure of something as compared to a larger one.[4] In Jesus' parable of the talents, one servant received five talents while another received only two. The distribution of the amount of "talents" that each of us has been given and blessed with was wholly contingent upon God's divine providence. Though the concept of two talents leadership derives from the premise of having received a smaller measure, its emphasis is not so much on the amount that was given but rather on the handling – the faithful stewardship of what was given. The concept of "Two Talents Leadership" predisposes the concept of faithful stewardship above all else. The concept focuses not on what we don't have but rather on what we do have. It doesn't focus on what we wished we had but on what God has already blessed us with. The concept of Two Talents Leadership elucidates how God is the owner, and we are merely stewards of His resources and blessings. The point of Two Talents Leadership is never a matter of how much we have been given but rather how well we use what we have been given. Stewardship is faithfully using all that God has entrusted to us for His purposes and glory.

Small churches oftentimes feel as if though they are limited in their resources like volunteers, money, and even talents and skills. The fact of the matter is God has equipped your small church with everything it needs to do exactly what He will call your church to accomplish. As faithful stewards, it is our job and responsibility to ensure that we take an accurate inventory of what we have been provided for by God and then determine exactly how to utilize those resources to maximize our impact in ministry for God's purposes and glory.

As tempting as it may be to want to do a lot more for the Lord, when we overextend ourselves and the resources that God has provided us, we actual show ourselves to be unfaithful in stewarding those resources well. To their own demise, small churches oftentimes have overextended themselves and their resources by trying to imitate the many and various programs and ministries that large churches have to offer. Small churches would do well by discerning and identifying the makeup of their unique ministry context and where they could make the most impact in the use of their available resources where they can get the most bang for their buck. Faithful small churches would do well to discover the one thing they do well where they could be the best that they could be and employ their resources there. In my first book, I share Harry and Esther Snyder's story about how they started In-N-Out Burger which continues to operate successfully by offering a simple menu of hamburgers.[5] They are known for doing this one thing – making the best burger in town! At least I think it's the best burger in town. What's the one thing that your small church can be the best at? Let God reveal that to you in prayer and discern it through your ministry context. Then when know what that is beyond a shadow of a doubt, put the resources that God has provided you into that one thing and do it well for the glory of God.

Faithfulness oftentimes requires patience and perseverance. The writer of the Book of Hebrews tells us to "run with perseverance the race marked out for us" (Heb 12:1). Oftentimes this race, which involves our faith and the ministry that God has called us to, is a slow and arduous process. Small church pastors and leaders should understand that the context of small church ministry can, should, and oftentimes is a slow process. This slow process is not characterized by a lack of results, but that the results are found in the process. It's not about a slick fast-paced process that produces substandard results but rather a slow intentional one that produces quality results. Oftentimes faithfulness is marked by a perseverance to do the slow and steady even when there are no evident results. It is sometimes and oftentimes a matter of faithfully doing what you've always done when you know it's what God is asking you to do despite a lack of tangible results. Instead of striving to achieve results that are a mile wide but only an inch deep, small churches should strive for results that are only an inch wide yet are a mile deep – quality over quantity.

Our ultimate goal in life and ministry is faithfulness. When I was an officer in the U.S. Marine Corps, we constantly used the phrase "Semper Fi!" The phrase is short for *semper fidelis* which is a Latin phrase adopted by the Marine Corps as its motto which means "always faithful." We should strive always to be faithful in our small church ministries. Our goal in the end is to hear the sweet words of our Lord say to us, "Well done, good and faithful servant. You have been faithful over a little; I will set you over much. Enter into the joy of your master" (Matt 25:27). Faithfulness is the overriding metric that the Lord will use to measure both the outcome of our lives and ministries.

CHAPTER 20
The Fruit

When it comes to gardening, fruit is one if not the most important goals. Fruit is the outcome or byproduct of the work of gardening; whether it is an incredibly beautiful rosebud or a wonderfully delectable peach, grape, or tomato. Fruit is the result of a healthy growing plant. The same is true for the small church; spiritual fruit is the result of a healthy small church. The fruit that the Bible refers to is a byproduct of the transformational work unto Christlikeness that the Holy Spirit is accomplishing in our lives. It is the character traits of love, joy, peace, forbearance, kindness, goodness, faithfulness, gentleness, and self-control (Gal 5:22-23). The Bible also considers fruit as people who come to the Lord through the witness and faithful obedience of our life in Christ (John 4:36, Rom 1:13, and 1 Cor 16:15). But here is the mysterious phenomenon about fruit – it is the result of a combination of the natural work of the gardener (i.e. tilling, planting, watering, fertilizing, etc.) and the supernatural work of "The Gardener." Take a look at this passage from John 15:1-11:

> [1]"I am the true vine, and my Father is the gardener. [2]He cuts off every branch in me that bears no fruit, while every branch that does bear fruit he prunes so that it will be even more fruitful. [3]You are already clean because of the word I have spoken to you. [4]Remain in me, as I also remain in you. No branch can bear fruit by itself; it must

remain in the vine. Neither can you bear fruit unless you remain in me.

[5]"I am the vine; you are the branches. If you remain in me and I in you, you will bear much fruit; apart from me you can do nothing. [6]If you do not remain in me, you are like a branch that is thrown away and withers; such branches are picked up, thrown into the fire and burned. [7]If you remain in me and my words remain in you, ask whatever you wish, and it will be done for you. [8]This is to my Father's glory, that you bear much fruit, showing yourselves to be my disciples.

[9]"As the Father has loved me, so have I loved you. Now remain in my love. [10]If you keep my commands, you will remain in my love, just as I have kept my Father's commands and remain in his love. [11]I have told you this so that my joy may be in you and that your joy may be complete.

This passage provides us with a good healthy perspective regarding the goal of producing fruit in our small churches. Though we play a role in the work of gardening, verse 1 tells us that our Heavenly Father is The Gardener, and He is the ultimate source and cause of all resulting fruit in our lives and ministries. Verses 2 and 8 tell us that fruit is an important aspect of our small church ministry because God wants for us to bear this fruit, for it brings glory to Him. Verses 4 and 5 tell us that we are incapable of bearing fruit unless we "remain" in Christ. What does it mean to "remain" in Christ? The word "remain" is from the Greek word *meno* which means to abide. Verse 7 tells us to allow Christ's words to remain or abide in us. This abiding process is allowing the truth of God's Word to fill our hearts, regulate our thoughts, direct our volitions, and transform our lives. In conjunction with verse 10, obedience to God's Word is a vital and essential component of this abiding process. Faithful obedience to live a life pleasing to and worthy of the Lord will cause us to bear fruit (Col 1:10). As we remain obedient to God's Word and the leading of the Holy Spirit in both our lives and our small churches, we will cultivate a life and ministry that will (super)naturally bear the fruit of the Holy Spirit. The essential addition of fruit that stems from our faith and obedience causes us and our small churches to be healthy and effective for kingdom work. Listen to Peter's words from 2 Peter 1:5-8, "For this reason, make every effort to add to your faith goodness; and to goodness, knowledge; and to knowledge, self-control; and to self-control, perseverance; and to perseverance, godliness; and to godliness, mutual affection; and to mutual affection, love. For if you possess these qualities in increasing measure, they will keep you from being ineffective and unproductive in your knowledge of our Lord Jesus Christ." The fruit produced by the Holy Spirit in our lives and small church ministries will ensure that we are neither ineffective nor unproductive. Effectiveness and productivity are also signs of church health.

As we and our small churches abide in Christ, we will bear fruit that is glorifying to God. In this abiding process, we are to remain faithful and obedient to God, and as a result we will bear fruit. What does this fruit look like in practical terms? At the end of this book, I provide you with a list of what I personally would consider descriptors of what good fruit looks like in a healthy small church. This list is not designed to be exhaustive nor comprehensive, but it is designed to give you a general idea of what to look for in determining whether or not you would consider your small church as being healthy. Good fruit in small church ministry is a good indication of health that is a result of a combination of the natural work of the people and the supernatural work of God.

CHAPTER 21
Conclusion (Section 3)

My dad loved gardening. He had the greenest thumb of anyone I have ever known. He made gardening look simple. He planted a garden at practically every single house he has ever lived in. At his last house in Las Vegas, he turned his entire backyard into a lush garden. He grew tomatoes, cucumbers, bell peppers, jalapeno peppers, bok choy, okra, green onions, eggplant, snow peas, string beans, apples, grapes, plums, figs, and Japanese pears. He spent a lot of time out in that garden. Even in his old age, my dad was out there in the backyard practically every day tending to his garden. Oftentimes when I came to visit him, we would spend a lot of time out in his garden either planting something new, watering what was growing, or just hanging out there talking about the good old days. My dad was in his element when he was out there gardening.

Unlike my dad, I couldn't grow anything if my life depended on it. Remember the story of the garden I had in the backyard of the first house I bought? Just recently my mother-in-law gave me an ashitaba plant which is suppose to hold nutrients in its leaves that is a source for various health remedies. The plant was in a pot that I kept on top of the kitchen counter next to both the window where it could get sunlight and next to the kitchen sink where I would water it. After a couple of months, the plant completely died. I'm not sure if I overwatered it or didn't give it enough water. Gardening never came easy for me as it did for my dad. On the other hand, gardening in the sense of ministry work has always been a complete joy for me. I definitely wouldn't say it was easy work, but it is definitely meaningful and rewarding.

Gardening in the spiritual sense takes on a variety of forms. The Bible refers to this as planting and watering, but this can look like serving, giving, loving, caring, and even encouraging. This is the role we play in God's great scheme of harvesting. As a small church, taking the focus off of growing the church has been a concept that I've advocated for and championed in my past couple of books. It has relieved small churches from the pressure of feeling responsible for something that they really do not have any control over. But they are still responsible for something – they are responsible for that part and aspect of ministry work which the Lord will call each of them to. This kind of spiritual gardening cultivates health in the small church. In Genesis 2:15 it says, "Then the Lord God took the man and put him in the garden of Eden to tend and keep it." This was before the Fall. Was it God's original design all along for us to do the work of gardening? We did it before the Fall to enjoy the fruit of our labor, and we still do it after the Fall to enjoy the fruit of our labor. When that work is done, then God causes good fruit to bear, and that fruit is a fairly good indication of a healthy small church. How does the fruit of your small church ministry fair? If you're questioning it (and the health of your small church), then grab some seeds, pick up a shovel or a watering can, and get to gardening – it's simple.

THE LIST

This is the list of what I would personally consider what "good fruit" looks like in a healthy small church. This list is not intended to be exhaustive but is designed to give you a general idea of whether or not your church would be considered healthy. The items are in no particular order.

1. There is a sense that the people in my small church genuinely love God.
2. There is a sense that the people in my small church sincerely love and care for one another.
3. The people in my small church have a heart to see lost people found.
4. The people in my small church have a heart to serve others.
5. The people in my small church are being transformed unto Christlikeness.
6. The people in my small church are sharing their faith and the gospel with others.
7. The people in my small church give generously to help others.
8. The people in my small church build close and meaningful relationships with one another.
9. There is a strong sense that the people in my small church depend on the power of the Holy Spirit to accomplish whatever God will call us to do as a small church.

10. Each person in my small church understands that they are important and valued.
11. The people in my small church strive to obey God.
12. God's Word is taught at my small church.
13. We pray a lot in my small church.
14. The people in my small church pray for each other.
15. Jesus is worshipped in my small church in more ways than just through music or singing.
16. Every person in my small church is recognized and celebrated.
17. We acknowledge people on their special days (i.e. birthdays, anniversaries, graduations, promotions, etc.) in my small church.
18. Spiritual growth and maturity is evident in the lives of the people in my small church.
19. Stewardship is considered important in my small church.
20. The pastor knows everyone's name (first and last) in my small church.
21. Everyone in my small church knows everybody else's name (first and last).
22. The pastor and the people in my small church know who is missing every Sunday.
23. I can call the pastor or any of the church leaders in my small church and receive counsel and prayer at anytime of the day.

24. I have fun being with and hanging out with the people in my small church.
25. The people in my small church hang out with each other outside the context of Sunday church gatherings.
26. I can trust my pastor and the church leaders with private personal issues in my life.
27. I have a real sense that the people in my small church are genuinely open and honest with me.
28. My small church is willing to help anyone in whatever way they can.
29. The people in my small church encourage one another.
30. The people in my small church lovingly admonish and correct each other.
31. The people in my small church are quick to forgive.
32. The people in my small church openly share their victories in Christ.
33. The people in my small church openly share their problems and struggles as well as their fears and doubts with one another.
34. The people in my small church laugh with one another.
35. The people in my small church cry with one another.
36. The people in my small church comprise of a variety of age groups.

37. Leaders are being developed in my small church.
38. I respect the leaders in my small church.
39. My small church works with other churches.
40. My small church financially supports overseas missionaries.
41. There is freedom to speak openly and honestly in my small church.
42. The people in my small church are kind, friendly and hospitable.
43. The people in my small church share how they work out their faith in situations outside of the context of Sunday church gatherings.
44. Guests feel welcomed in my small church, and the people in my church actually greet and talk with them.
45. I sense God's presence and power when the people of my small church gather together for God's purposes.
46. I sense that people are growing closer to God because of what my small church does.
47. There is a strong sense of community and family among the people in my small church.
48. The vision and mission of my small church is made clear.
49. My small church is looking to multiply.
50. Jesus is at the center of my small church.

INTERESTING NOTE: None of the items on this list can be measured numerically.

ENDNOTES
Section 3

1. Bob DeSagun, *Don't Supersize It! 10 Healthy Perspectives for the Small Church* (San Bernardino, CA: CreateSpace, 2015).

2. Bob DeSagun, *Two Talents Leadership: A Strategic Small Church Leadership Approach* (San Bernardino, CA: CreateSpace, 2015).

3. The Christian and Missionary Alliance Core Values (n.d.), retrieved from http://www.cmalliance.org/about/beliefs/values.

4. DeSagun, *Two Talents Leadership.*

5. DeSagun, *Don't Supersize It.*

SECTION 4
APPROACH

From the book
MORE THAN THREE SONGS
AND A SERMON
A Biblical Model For Small Church Ministry

Throughout history, culture has always been an influential factor in the development of the Christian community, yet aspects of the American culture have diminished and deteriorated what and how church was designed to be. The church that God so lovingly and sacrificially gave His Son to die for has been reduced to a mere event that is attended on Sunday mornings characterized by the singing of songs and the listening of a sermon. As a result, an onlooking world as well as the church's very own fledgling generations have been disenamored with what the church has become. In this book, Bob DeSagun helps to recapture some of the more ancient yet timeless principles and practices from Scripture that are easily adaptable in the small church.

CHAPTER 22
Introduction (Section 4)

I don't follow baseball, but once in a while I enjoy catching a live game at our local ballpark. It's a wonderful experience. It's fun, relaxing, and even exhilarating as long as the home team is winning. I even make it a point to try and catch a game when I'm traveling out of town. I have an unspoken goal to catch a major league baseball game at as many baseball parks as I can. The best part of the experience is the food. I love to grab a hot dog and some cotton candy. The green cotton candy, though rare to find, is the best! If you've never had green cotton candy, I would encourage you to make it one of your life's goals. It taste like Fruit Loops cereal. Baseball is America's favorite pastime. As Americans, we love to watch our sports. We have become a spectator sport nation. Spectator sports are a multibillion-dollar industry. It is only a small segment of our American entertainment industry.

We live in an entertainment culture, and the church has succumbed to the influence of this culture. Church has become a spectator sport in itself. Millions of spectators are gathering in "arenas" all across our nation on Sunday mornings to watch one of the greatest displays of Christian entertainment – we call it church. Our entertainment culture has invaded that space on Sunday morning that was once meant to be sacred but is now secular.

When we first planted the church here in San Diego, we adopted a typical model of doing church that you can probably find in any Christian church on any given Sunday morning. Like many Christian churches, we did not have our own building but instead rented a facility in the local community. Churches that rent facilities are commonly referred to as mobile churches – they bring everything they need into the rental facility to make church happen and pack up everything at the end. Like most mobile churches, we set up like any other typical Christian church; I call it auditorium or lecture style seating where rows of chairs are set up facing the front. When church started, the worship team led us in three songs and then I would come up and preach a sermon. People came in and took their seat, worship through the song set, listen to the sermon, and then headed home afterwards. That was the extent of church, at least how we did church. That's probably how most Christian churches do church on Sunday.

My intention is not to criticize how churches operate or function, nor is it my intention to advocate or promote one exclusive model or approach to church as superior. One thing I do believe is that what we do on Sunday morning when we gather should be the truest reflection of what church was designed to be. But I personally think that there's more to church than what we typically see or experience on any given Sunday morning. Church is more than a Sunday morning event where Christians come to gather, sing songs, listen to a sermon, and then go home. Unfortunately, that's what many perceive and expect church to be. Though they may not realize or confess it, many expect church to be an entertaining event. They expect a "band-like" worship team to rock the house with a concert-like experience. They expect the pastor or preacher to deliver an interesting, funny and entertaining message. In some churches, they expect at least some kind of video or live special performance. Though they may not admit or even realize it, people who attend are looking to come to be entertained. They come as spectators. But church was designed to be more than this. I often tell the people at our small church that church is more than three songs and a sermon. Church is so much more than just coming, singing three songs, listening to a sermon, and then just going home. I believe God designed church to be much more than our American culture has made it out to be.

Church was not designed to be a spectator sport but rather a participatory one. As much as I enjoy going and watching baseball games at the ballpark, I would much rather prefer to be playing the game instead. I'm more of a player than a spectator. I've always enjoyed playing sports. The church I pastor used to have a softball team that played in a local community league. We never won a game, but we sure did have a blast playing. We actually used it as an outreach opportunity to shine Jesus to the members of the other teams we played as well as to our community. At the end of every game, we would order pizza and hand out Gatorade and bottled water for the players of the other team.

I am not asserting that the model we use for ministry is the only model or even the right model for your church, but I do know that it is a biblical model. To think that there is one definitive model of church is absurd. God is trying to reach all different kinds of people with the gospel of His Son Jesus Christ, and it will take more than one model of church to accomplish that. The important thing to remember is that regardless of the model, we should remain uncompromising to the truths revealed to us in Scripture. The model of church will vary based on context, but we should adhere to the guidelines set for us in Scripture. The model that I present in this book is neither new nor innovative. I personally like to think of it as an ancient yet timeless biblical model.

In the preceding chapters, you will come across the boldface words *"At our small church"* near the end of every chapter. In these paragraphs, I provide you with some of the practices and approaches that have been successfully working in our unique context as a small church. This does not necessarily mean it will work for you, but I want to simply provide you with a model or approach to consider. I want to reaffirm that my intention is never to bash or bad-mouth other churches or the models or approaches they personally use. Each church is doing the best that she can to be the church that God is calling her to be in the unique context she finds herself in. It will take all of Jesus' churches working together in love and unity to fulfill The Great Commission.

CHAPTER 23
Gathering

Once a year I get to see all the members of my family at our annual family reunion dinner around the Thanksgiving holiday. It is one of the most highly anticipated times of the year for me personally. Most of my family members have ceded the actual Thanksgiving Day to spend the time with our spouse's family. Afterwards, we all would meet at my dad's house in Las Vegas to have our very own Thanksgiving meal on what is commonly known as Black Friday, but we called it "Thanksgiving Friday" in honor of the DeSagun family. I have aptly renamed it "DeSagiving." It's a time of feasting and family fun. My dad used to be a cook in the Navy. So every year he and my step-mom would cook and prepare food all day to ensure that we had an incredible spread that evening for dinner. The food was a fusion of traditional Thanksgiving food (i.e. turkey, stuffing, mashed potatoes, gravy, cranberry sauce, etc.) and Filipino cuisine served buffet style. It is your typical family reunion where everyone is just so excited to see one another. You can see, hear, feel and even smell and taste the love we have for one another at our Thanksgiving Friday family dinner gathering.

Church should be like a good ole family gathering. Church is about the gathering of the members of God's family. We have always referred to church as either God's people or the gathering of God's people. The purpose of the gathering of God's people as the church is two-fold: (1) discipleship – the spiritual growth, edification and encouragement of the church and (2) worship – the adoration and exaltation of Christ. In his epistle to the church in Corinth, the apostle Paul addressed some of the problems of the early church by providing them with some practical guidelines on how the church ought to function. Paul instructed the church that when they gathered, everything was to be done for the edification of the church (1 Cor 14:26). The writer of Hebrews not only warned Christians not to neglect gathering together but rather to encourage one another (Heb 10:25). The gathering was designed for the edification and encouragement of the church altogether. The gathering of God's people is also about worship. We'll talk more about this aspect of church in the next chapter, but worship was never about location. When Jesus addressed the Samaritan woman at the well in Sychar, He made a profound implication in regards to the proper location of worship. He told the woman, "...a time is coming when you will worship the Father neither on this mountain nor in Jerusalem" (John 4:21). Jesus explained that a new era has come (with Jesus and the new covenant) where temple worship was no longer a matter of physical location. Each believer was now considered the temple of the Holy Spirit (1 Cor 3:16). Jesus taught that "how" one worships was much more important than "where" one worships. Jesus taught that the "how" of worship is to be done "in Spirit and in truth" (John 4:23-24). Jesus taught that worship was a matter of the heart that encompassed the entirety of one's being. So whether you worship at your own church building or a rental facility like a school or community center, a coffee shop or restaurant, someone's house or even at a local public park is inconsequential.

The advantage of the small church is its ability to practically meet anywhere, but its real strength is the intimacy it fosters that result in close and meaningful relationships among its members. It is in these close and meaningful relationships where people find a sense of belonging. In his book *Shepherding the Small Church: A Leadership Guide for the Majority of Today's Churches*, Glenn Daman says, "In the small church, place is more important than location. The atmosphere that facilitates worship is not the beauty of the building or the aesthetics of the location, but the fact that each person has a place."[1] This intimate relational aspect of the small church's worship gathering builds connectivity, cohesiveness, and interdependence between its members. It is in these kinds of relationships that people find value and substance that adds to their faith and sense of community. In his book *Church 3.0: Upgrades for the Future Church*, Neil Cole says, "Relationships and spiritual connection become the valued currency rather than expensive buildings, technology, and promotional advertisements."[2]

At our small church, we have met at different venues and locales. Initially, we were in a rental facility for the first 10 years. Afterwards, we began to meet at a public beach park during the summer. During those summer months, we would set up four large canopy tents and duct tape them together to serve as our sanctuary and two separate ones with actual tent inserts for our children's ministries. We just asked our church members to either bring something to sit on like a beach chair, beach towel or blanket. Soon the public beach park became our church location for the most part of the year until the weather started getting cooler (in San Diego that would be around November). For the cooler months (November until May), we moved indoors into people's homes. We enjoyed the intimacy of the homes so much that we decided to move to the house church model and save money on the rental fee. We'll continue to do the house church model until the weather gets warmer, then we'll start meeting back at the public beach park.

When my dad passed away in 2012, my sister volunteered to open her home to host the annual "DeSagiving" gathering. She now has been doing this for the past couple of years. Last year I tried to convince my family to come down to San Diego where I offered to host our annual family gathering. Unfortunately, there were a lot of logistical challenges for some of my family members, so we just kept the location at my sister's house in Las Vegas. As much as I would have love the gathering to be in San Diego, the time we spent together continued to be amazing. Regardless of where the gathering was, we still had an incredible time together. The location was inconsequential. What mattered most was that we were getting together to see each other and to spend time together.

CHAPTER 24
Worship

Jesus' conversation with the Samaritan woman in Sychar reveals a great deal to us regarding worship. Jesus said, "God is spirit, and his worshipers must worship in the Spirit and in truth" (John 4:24). Jesus' response to the Samaritan woman reveals the true nature of authentic and genuine worship. Worshipping in spirit and truth involves the totality of the human essence created in the image of God (spirit) with an understanding of the revelation of God (truth). Worship is a responsive expression to God that is far beyond music or singing alone. I will not deny the meaning and impact that music has played throughout the Old Testament Scriptures and how the contemporary church has adapted it into its "worship service." Neither will I deny how music and singing can be a beautiful expressive form of how we worship God, but it is not the only form of worship. Worship is a spiritual response to the truth of God revealed in Scripture that is designed to prompt a sincere and wholehearted adoration grounded in a conviction of truth that originates from the spirit.

Worship is so much more than the songs we sing at church. Romans 12:1 says, "...to offer your bodies as a living sacrifice, holy and pleasing to God – this is your true and proper worship." The apostle Paul advocated that worship was not only a sacrificial offering unto God but it also encompasses the totality and whole being of a person and not just a manner of standing, clapping, singing, and lifting of hands (though all of these are suitable and expressive forms of biblical worship). Worship must not be limited to the time we sing in church. Worship is so much more. It is about offering the whole of our being as a holy sacrifice pleasing unto God. This is why the apostle Paul said to offer our bodies – all of us – as a living sacrifice. True and proper worship is the way we live our lives every day in every way in sacrifice to and honor of God. Worship is about serving, sharing and caring. Worship is about eating, breathing and sleeping. Worship is about playing and working. It's about how we treat our spouse and how we raise our kids. It's about how we spend our time and money. It's about admiring and adoring. It's about stewardship and faithfulness. It's about humility and thankfulness. It's about joy and celebration. It's about love and service. It's about what we think, what we say, and what we do. We were created and designed to worship, so everything we do is about worship.

Worship is also about what we offer to God. Worship is a sacrificial offering or gift that we bring and give to God in adoration of Him. In 1 Corinthians 12, the apostle Paul presents a list of spiritual gifts (others which are also listed in Romans 12). This list was not meant to be exhaustive. Then in the context of this list of spiritual gifts, Paul explains in 1 Corinthians

14:26 that when we gather as a church, we are to use these gifts for the edification and encouragement of the whole church. The gifts we bring and use in our small church gatherings are considered forms and expressions of our worship to God. If someone brings a teaching, then their teaching is considered a gift of worship. If someone brings a song or hymn (or sings), then their song or hymn (or singing) is considered a gift of worship. If someone brings a prayer, then their prayer is considered a gift of worship. I will even go as far as to say that simply coming to church is considered a gift of worship. Worship is what we sacrifice and bring as an offering to honor God.

At our small church, we have experimented with various approaches to worship. There are times when we would lead in traditional worship (led by someone playing a guitar for a couple of songs). There are times when we would sing acapella for worship. Lately, we have encouraged people to share why or how a particular worship song has ministered to them personally, then we would play the song off of someone's iPhone connected via Bluetooth to an external speaker. Sometimes people sing along and worship and other times they'll just listen and reflect and meditate on the lyrics as worship. Does this mean you have to have music and sing in order to worship? Of course not. There are times when we don't have any music or singing at all in our gatherings. We'll use moments of solitude to worship God. We'll use prayer to worship God. We'll use the reading of God's Word (especially the Book of Psalms) to worship Him. I just recently met with a pastor friend of mine who shared with me how they too have done away with traditional worship that is led by a band or worship team. He explained to me how (to be quite frank) their musical and singing talent was not up to par. He told me that their worship leader would sing in a different note or key than what the musicians were actually playing in. This created such a dissonance that it became more of a distraction to the worship experience, so he simply did away with this traditional approach and moved towards a more instrumental and expressive one. Experimenting with worship can be fun and profound. One time, I asked a young lady to sit at the center of our gathering (we sit "in the round" facing each other in a circle rather than auditorium or lecture style), then I asked members of the church to share how they appreciate her by saying nice things to her or by simply complimenting her. People told her how much they admired her for her love and care for others. Others expressed her how much they appreciate her faithful service to the church. Others complimented her on how beautiful she looked. Then I had her sit back in her original seat while leaving the chair in the middle of our gathering empty. Then I instructed the church to close their eyes and imagine that God was sitting in that chair in the middle. I further instructed them to say whatever they wanted to say to God as if though He were actually sitting in that chair. Immediately, they began to admire God for His love and care for them. Others expressed how much they appreciated Him for his faithfulness to them. Others thanked Him for all of His provisions and blessings. Others complimented on how beautiful He is. It was one of the most powerfully raw and emotionally authentic worship times that we have ever experienced. The fact of the matter was God was really there. Maybe He wasn't sitting on that chair, but He was definitely there listening to each of our expressions of worship.

Music is only one of many expressions of worship. Worship is about the way we live our lives sacrificially in honor of God. It is the most appropriate response to the revelation of the truth of God. It is aided by the Spirit and exalts the Savior. It expands from the menial to the majestic and encompasses every aspect of our lives. It is comes from the core of who we were designed and created to be in relation to God, and it is so much more than just singing at church.

CHAPTER 25
Sermon

Preaching is a vital component not only in evangelism and discipleship but also in bringing back the Savior King. In Matthew 24:14, Jesus said, "And this gospel of the kingdom will be preached in the whole world as a testimony to all nations, and then the end will come." Throughout the Book of Acts we see the gospel message and God's Word being preached. The apostle Paul instructs Timothy to preach the Word (2 Tim 4:2). Preaching is unique in that it is designed to elicit a response from its audience. When God's Word or the gospel message is preached, it elicits a response to act. That act can be one of repentance, obedience, or faith. Preaching is designed to proclaim truth that elicits an action or response. God's Word has that affect on its hearers. Because of this, the sermon has become the central component of the worship service – and rightfully so because it is designed to proclaim God's Word which in turn is designed to reveal Jesus the Christ (John 5:39).

But the American entertainment and consumerist culture has morphed the preaching of God's Word into more of a performance. The preaching of God's Word has been evaluated on how eloquent and clever pastors or preachers have creatively and entertainingly crafted their sermons to engage their audience. It is an art we commonly refer to as homiletics. I find it interesting that the apostle Paul says, "And so it was with me, brothers and sisters. When I came to you, I did not come with eloquence or human wisdom as I proclaimed to you the testimony about God. For I resolved to know nothing while I was with you except Jesus Christ and him crucified. I came to you in weakness with great fear and trembling. My message and my preaching were not with wise and persuasive words, but with a demonstration of the Spirit's power, so that your faith might not rest on human wisdom, but on God's power" (1 Cor 2:1-5). I don't deny the need for diligent study, sermon prep and a homiletics that is designed to prevent ambiguity and maximize clarity in properly and even strategically proclaiming and communicating the truth of God's Word. Done properly, preaching should be an outflow of the life of the pastor/preacher. In his book *Power Through Prayer*, E. M. Bounds says, "The man – the whole man – lies behind the sermon. Preaching is not the performance of an hour; it is the outflow of a life. It takes twenty years to make a sermon because it takes twenty years to make the man. The true sermon is a thing of life."[3] The sermon should be a byproduct of prayer. Bounds also says, "The real sermon is made in the prayer closet."[4] People need sermons that are packed with the Word of God and aided by the power of the Holy Spirit because prayer went before it that will transform lives not with psychobabble, shallow anecdotes, famous quotes, stories or jokes that merely entertain.

The sermon is not the only effective means of the ministry of God's Word. For a large church it may be the most effective and convenient way to communicate God's Word; but for the small church, participatory meetings where members contribute towards the ministry of God's Word in discussion and the encouraging of each other's faith is not only an effective model but also a biblical one. The apostle Paul's instructions from 1 Corinthians 14:26 can easily be applied to participatory meetings. In participatory meetings, any member can contribute in the use of their spiritual gifts towards the overarching purpose of edifying and encouraging the whole church. In this type of model and approach, one can bring a teaching that is facilitated through a discussion where any and/or all can participate. In a discussion format, comments can be added and questions can be asked. The participatory meeting gets people discussing and talking about God's Word in an interactive manner that is enhanced with community involvement. It has been said that people remember 20 percent of what they hear but 70 percent of what they say. So why not get them saying God's Word in a participatory setting rather than simply hearing a sermon preached? Why not get them interacting with others in the discussion of God's Word rather than just hearing God's Word preached week after week? That way they retain more of God's Word.

I would also caution and encourage pastors and church leaders to lovingly, respectfully and sensitively address any errancies with teachings and discussions that take place in participatory gatherings that are not in line with God's Word. It is the pastor and church leaders' responsibility not only to teach but also to rebuke and correct when necessary (2 Tim 3:16).

I am not against sermons being preached, but I have discovered the advantages for the discussion of God's Word between church members that promotes relational discipleship, community, care and trust. People don't need another sermon. What they need is a community that they can trust with their questions, fears and doubts, and that will encourage them in their faith. This can be accomplished through a participatory meeting where individuals can freely share as well as be heard and understood.

The unique aspect of the participatory meeting is how each member has the opportunity to contribute towards the encouragement and edification of the church. In lieu of a song set accompanied by a sermon that is typically found in a traditional church service, the participatory meeting allows for individuals to be a part of the ministering that is happening. The participatory meeting values each member for not only who they are but the gift that they bring collectively and collaboratively towards the building up and edification of the church. When we started the participatory meeting approach at our church, I brought a kid's shape puzzle to illustrate the concept from 1 Corinthians 14:26. The kid's puzzle I used was the wooden kind that was designed to teach kids how to fit the different colored shaped puzzle pieces into their respective matching slots. Before we started church, I would hand out a puzzle piece to each member and instruct them that they were only able to put their puzzle piece into its matching slot only after they contributed in some way toward the participatory meeting either by teaching, adding to the discussion through a comment or question, sharing a song or a testimony, praying, hosting the church gathering at their home, or by providing the fellowship meal (which we'll talk more about in the next chapter). Once they contributed to the participatory meeting, they were allowed to place their puzzle piece into its perspective slot on the puzzle board. I explained how each of them represented the puzzle pieces – how each of them is different in color and shape and how those unique differences represented the spiritual gifts that each of them possessed. I further explained that when they operated in their unique spiritual gift and contributed towards the participatory meeting for the building up and edification of the church, we symbolically fit our unique and distinct puzzle piece in its matching slot that contributes towards the completion and wholeness of the puzzle. When each member plays their part as they obediently operate in their unique spiritual gifts in the participatory meeting, they each contribute to the edification, growth and wholeness of the church (Eph 4:16).

At our small church, we do not limit the contribution of what each person brings to just spiritual gifts. We encourage people to bring and share whatever and however the Lord would lead them as long as the end goal is for the encouragement and edification of the whole church. What they bring is their unique and special gift and offering of worship to God. The collective contributions of what every person brings creates the worship atmosphere. Someone will offer their home to meet in as their offering, another will bring a song or hymn to share or lead in singing, another will bring a testimony or story of God's goodness and faithfulness, another will bring a teaching, while others participate and add to the discussion with their comments and/or questions, others will pray, while others will merely consider simply being there as their offering (Rom 12:1). We have a young girl who loves to bake, and she would bake something delicious and bring it to church as an offering of worship to God for all of us to enjoy. There are still times when I as the pastor feel led to preach a sermon, but lately this occurrence has been rare. There are even times when we would devote the entire participatory meeting for prayer or just for sharing testimonies and faith stories that glorify God and encourage others. We have found that the members of our church take active roles in ministering to one another during this time of our gathering as oppose to just sitting there and listening to me preach a sermon. It brings new life to the phrase "the priesthood of all believers."

The participatory meeting facilitates an environment where all can belong and be a part of. The participatory meeting is inclusive. It respects and celebrates each individual for who they are and what they bring to the worship gathering collectively and collaboratively towards the encouragement and edification of the whole church. The participatory meeting cultivates an environment where everybody is important and where everybody matters (1 Cor 12:21). It doesn't promote nor single out any "celebrity" personalities because Jesus is the only celebrity at church who should be exalted.

CHAPTER 26
Food

I love food! On my Facebook profile, I posted that my all-time favorite quote in the whole wide world is from the late S. Truett Cathy, founder of Chic-fil-A, who said, "Food is essential to life; therefore, make it good." I use to be one of those kinds of people on Facebook who would post pictures of food. For whatever reason, I would take a picture of my food and let the whole social media world know what I was eating at that very moment. I posted pictures of my meal, my desserts, my snacks, and even my drinks like coffee or boba (my Asian friends know what I talking about). I'm a foodie, so what can I say? I had one of my friends on Facebook tell me that she was surprised that I wasn't like 400 pounds heavier with all the food pictures that I post. It wasn't until one of my other friends told me that I post quite a bit of food pictures. That's when I realized how true it was. At that moment, I stopped posting the food pictures. Then all of a sudden I received a rash of posts on my Facebook timeline from friends who were asking me what happened and why wasn't I posting food pictures anymore? I told them I was a bit ashamed of all the food pictures I had been posting. They responded back by saying how much they missed seeing my food picture posts. One friend told me that she would look on my timeline to see what food pictures I posted so as to give her ideas on what to have for dinner that evening. Right then and there, I started the food picture posts again. I don't post them as much now, but I still love food!

Food is amazing! It is essential in order to sustain life. Even Jesus said, "Man shall not live on bread alone, but from every word that comes from the mouth of God" (Matt 4:4). He knew the importance of partaking God's Word, but He also understood the necessity of food. But I believe that there is something more to food than just merely the physical. There exists a deep spiritual connection when people share a meal together.

Meal sharing was evident throughout the New Testament. It is evident throughout Jesus' ministry. He ate with tax collectors and sinners (Matt 9:11), and His last meal was with His disciples (Matt 26:20-21). The early church "broke bread" together, and this was not a reference to the mere juice and wafer that we partake of when we observe communion or the Lord's Supper; it was the sharing of a whole meal together. Sharing a meal together was one of the most characteristic practices of the early church gatherings (Acts 2:42, 1 Cor 11:17-22 and Jude 12). Even the completed work of our faith through the redemptive work of our Lord culminates in heaven with the wedding feast of the Lamb (Rev 19:7-10) – a grand and glorious celebration depicted as a "feast" (I believe this to be literal rather than symbolic).

The shared meal was characteristic of apostolic worship and of the early Christian churches that met in homes. Though it was closely related to the practice of the Lord's Supper, it was a distinctive and entirely different practice that involved the sharing of an entire meal together. The practice was commonly referred to as the *agape* or *love feast* and continued in church gatherings throughout the second and third centuries. Some scholars assert that the practice was done away with as church gatherings became too large to accommodate such meals and was thus replaced entirely by the practice of just communion. The shared meal was a symbol of affiliation for those who proclaimed faith in the Risen Savior and was an expression of their common unity. In his book *Paul's Idea of Community: The Early House Churches in Their Cultural Setting*, Robert Banks says, "This meal is vital, for as the members of the community eat and drink together their unity comes to visible expression."[5] Jesus said, "I have given them the glory that you gave me, that they may be one as we are one - I in them and you in me – so that they may be bought to complete unity. Then the world will know that you sent me and have loved them even as you have loved me" (John 17:22-23). The fellowship meal is a unique and distinctive expression of the unity of the Christian community.

At our small church, we provide a fellowship meal every time we gather as a church. As a house church, we no longer pay a rental fee every Sunday for our meeting space, so we have now allocated those funds towards providing a fellowship meal every time we gather. We have asked the host family to provide the fellowship meal for that Sunday's gathering. The food choice is at the discretion of the host family; so as a multicultural church, we have the incredible blessing to experience a wide variety of ethnic foods. So on any given Sunday, we might have Chinese, Filipino, Indian, or American cuisine. Most of the time, our hosts for church will provide a home-cooked meal and at other times will cater in from a local restaurant. Sometimes we all just go out to a local restaurant together and the church will pick up the check. Either way, a fellowship meal is provided every Sunday. One distinctive advantage of providing a fellowship meal is the extended time of fellowship and ministry that happens when we continue to gather. Church (the participatory meeting) will start at 11:00am and end at 12:00 noon, and afterwards we'll have the fellowship meal (typically lunch). The last person will leave anywhere between 2:30 and 4:30pm. Regardless of the end time, the extended fellowship that is facilitated by providing a meal is opportunity for more organic ministry to take place. During this extended time of fellowship, we see people build close and meaningful relationships, people pray for each other, further discussion on the teaching topic from the participatory meeting occurs, questions are asked and answers are found, testimonies and faith stories are shared, people are counseled, relational discipleship happens, and people are encouraged and inspired in their faith. And the pastor isn't doing it all!

Sharing a meal together provides a wonderful opportunity for ministry to happen that would not normally happen in a typical church service where there's just the singing of songs and the listening of a sermon. The meal creates a place of both intimacy and unity where relationships are strengthened, guards and walls are let down, openness, honesty, and vulnerability take place which allows for wonderful and powerful ministry to happen among God's people for God's purposes. Don't underestimate the power of food!

CHAPTER 27
Community

God has designed for us to live in community. We see this concept inherent in the Godhead. He is a relational God and exists in community; a community that we commonly refer to as The Trinity. Even the relational titles He has chosen to depict Himself throughout the Scriptures are that of family (Father and Son). God has designed the church to be a community that is much more characteristic of family (Eph 2:19 and 1 Thes 4:10). This family dimension of community is evidenced throughout the apostle Paul's epistles in his use of familial terms such as father, mother, brother and sister in relation to other members of the church. Community breeds a sense of family.

The name of our church (Experience Church) comes from 1 John 1:3 from The Message version of the Bible. There you'll find it say, "We saw it, we heard it, and now we're telling you so you can *experience* it along with us, this *experience* of communion with the Father and his Son, Jesus Christ" (1 John 1:3 MSG italics mine). The word "experience" is originally the Greek word *koinonia* which means fellowship or community. Koinonia is best understood in the words "one another" as it appears throughout the New Testament Scriptures. It says to be devoted to one another (Rom 12:10), honor one another (Rom 12:10), live in harmony with one another (Rom 12:16 and 1 Pet

3:8), accept one another (Rom 15:7), serve one another in love (Gal 5:13), be kind and compassionate to one another (Eph 4:32), admonish one another (Col 3:16), bear one another's burdens (Gal 6:2), encourage one another (1 Thes 5:11 and Heb 3:13), spur one another on toward love and good deeds (Heb 10:24), offer hospitality to one another (1 Pet 4:9), and love one another (1 Pet 1:22, 1 John 3:11, 3:23, 4:7, and 4:11-12). Christian community is about devotion and commitment – devotion and commitment to God and one another. In his book, Robert Banks wrote regarding the apostle Paul's view of community that, "He not only proclaimed the message about Christ and brought people into an intimate relationship with God, but he also explained the consequences of that message for the life of his converts and led them into a personal relationship with one another. As we have seen, for Paul the gospel bound believers to one another as well as to God."[6] The Scriptures call believers into devoted community to one another. A person outside of Christian community (church) is a person outside of the will of God.

Community is one of the most defining characteristics of church, yet it is all too often diminished when Christians fail to devote themselves fully to God and one another. Christians will either come to church, sing three songs and listen to a sermon and then they'll go home, or they'll simply forsake going to church altogether (Heb 10:25). The ones who attend and leave with no community interaction oftentimes perceive church as a religious duty to check off their list for the week. The only community interaction they engage in is that very brief moment in service when the pastor instructs the whole congregation to greet one another right before he begins preaching his sermon. The moment service ends, they head straight for the exit. God designed community to be so much more than this, but we've reduced it to a mere event that takes place in an hour on Sunday morning.

Community is about a whole-hearted devotion to God and one another. This is best seen in the early New Testament church in Acts 2:42-47:

> They devoted themselves to the apostles' teaching and to fellowship, to the breaking of bread and to prayer. Everyone was filled with awe at the many wonders and signs performed by the apostles. All the believers were together and had everything in common. They sold property and possessions to give to anyone who had need. Every day they continued to meet together in the temple courts. They broke bread in their homes and ate together with glad and sincere hearts, praising God and enjoying the favor of all the people. And the Lord added to their number daily those who were being saved.

The early Christian believers were devoted to their community. They were devoted to God and to each other for the well-being and spiritual formation of one another. Their devotion to one another cultivated a community of love, care, concern, and worship. It was a community that helped when one of their members stumbled (Ecc 4:10), and it was a community where they all suffered and rejoiced together (1 Cor 12:26). Their devotion and commitment to one another was a breeding ground for both unity and relational discipleship.

In our small church, we function as a family. We try and think along the lines of "what would family do?" If a member of our church had a birthday or anniversary, it was a means for celebration. We made sure that every member was celebrated and received (at the very least) a birthday card and gift card to Baskin-Robbins for their birthday. If someone were running late for church (and we knew they were on their way), then we would wait for them before we started. We've had members of our church who work on Sundays, so we've moved church gatherings to another evening of the week to accommodate them into fellowship. We have a couple of vegetarians in our church, so we think about them when we prepare our fellowship meals. These might seem like small things, but you'll be surprise how much they mean to those whom we think about. We always try to consider every member of our church when we make decisions. Nobody is left out, and everybody has a voice or say in the matter. These small gestures are indications of the love and care that is magnified when the real big storms of life happen, and we as a community are there for one another.

Christian community is a foretaste of the kingdom of God. It extends far beyond a mere hour on Sunday morning. It is a gathering where the reign of God manifests the character of His kingdom among its citizens. It is a gathering where the presence of God is felt and the power of God is experienced. It is a gathering where people are devoted to God and one another. It is a gathering characterized by love, joy, peace, rest and celebration. It is an inclusive community where all are welcomed, and all can find a family to belong and be a part of. It is a gathering where people find healing, forgiveness, hope, encouragement and inspiration. It is a gathering where Jesus is worshipped, exalted and glorified. It is a gathering of God's people where the practice of "one another" is prevalent.

CHAPTER 28
Accountability

Recently a well-known technology company engaged into a major legal battle against a government law enforcement agency regarding the privacy issues of one of their customers. The company fought a federal court order to provide access to information contained in one of their customer's products as a precedent regarding due process and privacy laws. The influence of individualism in American culture affects our attitude and viewpoints regarding our privacy. We all value privacy. We want our lives to be private. We want our business to be our business alone. We want our secrets to remain secrets. What happens behind closed doors stays behind closed doors – in other words, "What happens in Vegas, stays in Vegas." We all have skeletons in our closets. Yet these skeletons continue to enslave us.

Church should be a place where people can find freedom from these skeletons and live in the victorious power of Christ. God empowers His people through the Holy Spirit as well as through Christian accountability to stand against temptations and live victoriously through Christ. Christian accountability cultivates relationships where humility and vulnerability is practiced (Eph 4:2), sin is lovingly and gracefully dealt with (Gal 6:1), and where spiritual formation and growth is refined (Prov 17:17). Christian accountability also provides a loving and nonjudgmental environment for people to come and confess their sins and find healing in the Lord (James 5:16). Christians fail to realize and understand the power behind accountability; instead, they shy away from environments that promote accountability for fear of shame, guilt, and judgment. Other Christians view accountability as a burden like any other spiritual discipline that they chose not to practice because of a lack of commitment.

It is inevitable to not be accountable in a small church. Because of the size of the small church, intimacy and authenticity is easily cultivated which causes care and concern for one another that results in openness and honesty among its members. Close and meaningful relationships cause accountability to develop through genuine love and care for one another. Shame and guilt are replaced by community that promotes healthy interdependence and interconnectedness between its members resulting in freedom and empowerment.

At our small church, if someone were missing from any of our gatherings, we would call them to make sure that they're ok. We are not legalistic about weekly church attendance, but the accountability aspect cultivates a genuine care and concern among members of our small church. We check up on each other periodically either by visiting, calling, e-mailing or texting to ensure that each of us are doing well. We make it a habit to ask how we can pray for one another and then actually pray. We also diligently follow up with one another regarding each other's prayer requests. I make it a habit to ask people "How are you doing?" And then after they say, "Fine," I ask them, "But how are you really doing?" We express how much we really care for each other. We want to cut through the facades we typically put on and get to the real issues. We cultivate an atmosphere and environment of trust by keeping information that is shared with us confidential unless we have been given permission to share it with others. We let our guards down by being open and honest with each other as we share our challenges, temptations, struggles, doubts, fears, failures, and shortcomings. Most importantly, we try to just be real, authentic and transparent as possible.

Accountability is a powerful element of church that is oftentimes avoided by its members. We find ourselves uncomfortable in sharing our deepest darkest secrets yet accept living in enslavement that results in depression, discouragement, and defeat. The small church fosters an environment for accountability to lovingly and naturally take place – an accountability that dissolves guilt and shame by liberating and empowering. I came across an anonymous quote online that said, "You either make yourself accountable or you will be made accountable for your circumstances." Isn't this so true in light of Romans 14:12? Christian accountability is about deeper relational commitments resulting in spiritual growth and maturity in Christ.

CHAPTER 29
Missions

After my commission as an officer in the Marine Corps, I attended a six month long intensive officer basic infantry training commonly known as The Basic School (TBS) in Quantico, Virginia. TBS is where all newly commissioned Marine Corps officers are taught the basics of being an "officer of Marines." This included, but was not limited to, leadership, weapons, land navigation, rifle squad, platoon tactics, and expeditionary operations training. TBS taught the Marine officer the basic skills for combat. It was at TBS where I was introduced to the acronym "SMEAC." SMEAC is a five-paragraph field order that helps a Marine organize tactical information regarding military situations in order to help understand and execute a mission. The letter "S" stands for situation – What is your current situation? What kind of weather are you facing? What kind of terrain must be traversed? The letter "M" stands for mission – What have you been assigned to accomplish? The letter "E" stands for execution – How will you accomplish the mission? The letter "A" stands for administration and logistics – What supplies and equipment do you have available at your disposal? And the letter "C" stands for command and control – What lines of communication do you have? We were taught that every aspect of "SMEAC" has the potential to change in combat at any given moment except for one – the mission. The mission never changes. As soldiers in the Lord's army, our mission never changes either. We have received our marching orders from the Lord, and they will not change.

God is on mission to redeem our lost and fallen world. God has been working out His plan long before any of us. He has invited us be a part of His redemptive plan (1 Cor 3:9 and John 17:18). We have the opportunity to come alongside God and be a part of His eternal work. Our mandate of The Great Commission is to go and make disciples (Matt 28:19), but like worship, the fulfillment of this mandate takes the entirety of the way we live our lives before an onlooking world. Our lives are meant to be witnesses to others that testify of a Risen and Living Savior.

The fulfillment of The Great Commission requires the obedience of every believer to faithfully play his or her role and trust that God will play His (1 Cor 3:6). This is our great privilege, honor and responsibility. The roles and opportunities that each of us will play will vary throughout our faith journey. There will be times when God will ask us to pray for someone or to reach out to someone. There might be a time when God will ask us to share our faith story. God might ask us to financially support a missionary overseas or serve in a local organization to help others who are less fortunate. He might ask us to teach our kids His precepts or honor and cherish our spouse.

He'll even ask us to share the gospel message of Jesus Christ and invite someone towards repentance and salvation. Whatever God will ask us to do is all part of His mission. The mission will not only affect the lives of others but ours as well.

Missions is more than just an event or program that a church puts on. Missions, like worship, is about how we live our lives in honor of God and as a witness for Christ. Oftentimes we view missions as what we do to reach and win people over to the gospel, but missions goes beyond this. Though conversion is an important part of missions, it is not the only part. I wonder how many thousands upon thousands of people have made decisions for Jesus but have failed to be properly discipled into a growing and maturing relationship with Christ. In his book *Transforming Discipleship: Making Disciples A Few At A Time*, Greg Oden says, "We often perpetuate superficiality by casting a wider net, without the commensurate depth."[7] According to Ogden, "Disciples cannot be mass produced. We cannot drop people into a program and see disciples emerge at the end of the production line. It takes time to make disciples. It takes individual personal attention."[8] This is where the small church has a unique advantage to provide intimate relationships among its members that facilitate personal relational discipleship. In his book *The Small Church in the Mind of God: A Noumenological Perspective*, Dr. Emory James says, "When one considers the commission it should be noted

217

that the mandate of discipleship can more easily be met out of intimacy."[9]   Mission requires deep and meaningful relational connections that foster and cultivate discipleship.   Oftentimes the mission of discipleship is slow, long and arduous work.   In his book *The Master Plan of Evangelism*, Robert Coleman says, "The only hope for the world is for laborers to go to them with the gospel of salvation, and having won them to the Savior, not to leave them, but to work with them faithfully, patiently, painstakingly, until they become fruitful Christians savoring the world about them with the Redeemer's love."[10]   Small churches are uniquely situated to provide an intimate environment where deep relationships are cultivated and spiritual formation and maturity in Christ happens organically.

At our small church, we teach a philosophy of ministry that we personally refer to as "In-N-Out" (coincidentally that happens to be my favorite hamburger joint).   In-N-Out refers to "growing in community" and "living out mission."   We teach that every time we gather as a church on a weekly basis, we encourage and inspire each other to grow spiritually together as a community. We learn to grow in our faith and love God and one another. Then when we leave our church gatherings, we "live out mission" in the context of our everyday lives.   Instead of doing outreach and evangelism "events" put on by the church only a few times a year, we live out outreach and evangelism in our lives and in our unique and distinctive contexts 365 days a year. We teach and encourage people to live missionally in the unique contexts of their lives – whether at home, work, or in their community. We teach them that the roles they play in their families and with their friends, at their places of employment, and in their neighborhoods and communities where they live are all a part of their call to missions work. We teach them to adopt the posture, thinking, behaviors, and practices of a missionary in order to engage others with the gospel right where they're at. It communicates the reason for Christian living – partnering with God on His mission in the world to bring about His kingdom. We do this by loving, praying for, spending time with, and serving others who are far away from God. We teach people that God has already been at work in these people's lives way before we entered into it, and we now have the privilege and opportunity to add to what God has already started and will finish. We teach them how to naturally and organically fulfill the mandate of The Great Commission daily. In his book *Organic Outreach for Ordinary People: Sharing Good News Naturally*, Kevin Harney says, "Organic outreach is about living the kind of life that naturally draws people to Jesus. It involves speaking the kinds of words that you use in ordinary conversations and that reveal the presence of a loving God. It means loving people in a way that is genuine. Organic outreach is all about sharing our faith in a way that is authentic, real, and feels natural to the people around us."[11] Living out mission should be synonymous with everyday Christian living. We encourage members of our small church to connect with and serve in organizations where they can live out mission based on their interests. As a small church, we no longer create outreach ministries and programs; instead, we connect our members with organizations that have a track record for what they do best. Larger churches provide its members with a variety of ministries and programs that are well staffed and resourced for outreach and evangelism in the local community. Small churches should be encouraged to connect with larger churches and serve their community through such programs. There are also numerous national and local organizations (though not necessarily faith-based) that provide incredible opportunities for Christians to serve their community. As our church members serve in various ways throughout their neighborhoods and communities, they invite other members of the church to join or support them. Our church's associate pastor and his wife serve refugee families through a local organization in our city, and they have invited members of our church to help. They have also invited the refugee families to our church gatherings as well. We also have a member of our church that works for Volunteers of America, and we try to connect other members of our church and our resources to support and serve through them. Sometimes in our weekly church gatherings, we'll break up into small groups of three or four people and share how the Lord has led each of us to live missionally with the very people that God has already placed in our lives. We learn from each other how to naturally engage our family, friends, and coworkers with the gospel. Then we'll pray for those people in our groups. We'll also have a follow-up time and share how God is working in the lives of the people they prayed for, interacted with, and served.

God is a Missional God. He has allowed each of us an incredibly privileged opportunity to be a part of His redemptive mission in the world. Missional living is about bringing people who are far away from God closer to Him. As we help to accomplish this, we discover that we ourselves are drawing closer and closer to God. The mission not only affects the lives of the countless number of people that God is trying to reach but also affects our lives as well. We'll find no greater meaning for our lives here on earth than when we partner on mission with God.

CHAPTER 30
Conclusion (Section 4)

I love my wife. I have an intense and indescribable love for her. She means the world to me. We have been married for over 25 years, and every year my love for her grows more and more. There is nothing more that I'd rather do than to be with my wife and spend time with her. I value her. I cherish her. I love her. I would do anything to express how much I love her. Without a second thought, I would give my life for her. As much as I love my wife, I know that my love for her pales in comparison with the love that Christ has for His church (Eph 5:25). The love that Jesus has for His church depicts how precious the church is to Him. Why would we treat her (the church) any less? Why would we minimize her to what takes place within an hour on a Sunday morning?

The church is an assembly of God's people for His purpose. Many things take place in that assembly – worship, singing, the reading of God's Word, preaching, teaching, prayer, the Lord's Supper, and fellowship. These things were all designed to be pieces of a puzzle that capture the essence of God's kingdom here on earth. Individually these things are meaningful but collectively they become priceless. They create a sacred space in our world that gives us a glimpse for what our aching hearts long for – a heavenly country. The church is a hospital where the sick find healing and hope and a family where the orphaned and abandoned find a place to belong. It is the manifested movement of God's Spirit through willing and obedient vessels for the execution and fulfillment of God's redemptive plan here on earth.

Church is so much more than what happens within a time span of an hour or so on any given Sunday morning. Church is so much more than what we have made it out to be. We have inadvertently allowed aspects of our American culture to diminish and deteriorate its true essence and design. But we can recapture these ancient and timeless practices that are demonstrated throughout the pages of the New Testament. Maximizing what happens within that hour or so on Sunday morning is vital to the meaning and purpose of what church is all about – one that testifies of the heavenly goodness and grace of a Merciful and Loving God. In their book *Church Turned Inside Out: A Guide for Designers, Refiners, and Re-Aligners*, Linda Bergquist and Allan Karr say, "We are suggesting that what our local church becomes in structure and model should come from an intersection of scriptural principles, a passionate understanding of who we personally are in Christ, understanding and love for our macrocommunity, and the distinctive characteristics and accountability of our microcommunity – and ultimately an expression of Jesus' principle of the Kingdom of God."[12]

For the small church, we have been uniquely situated to adapt these scriptural principles back into our gatherings. It's time to recapture the true essence of what God has designed His church to be. We may only have an hour on any given Sunday morning; so therefore, let us use it wisely.

ENDNOTES
Section 4

1. Glenn Daman, *Shepherding the Small Church: A Leadership Guide for the Majority of Today's Churches* (Grand Rapids, MI: Kregel Publications, 2008).
2. Neil Cole, *Church 3.0: Upgrades for the Future Church* (San Francisco, CA: Jossey-Bass, 2010).
3. E. M. Bounds, *Power Through Prayer* (Kensington, PA: Whitaker House, 1982).
4. Ibid, 16.
5. Robert J. Banks, *Paul's Idea of Community: The Early House Churches in Their Cultural Setting* (Grand Rapids, MI: Baker Academic, 1994).
6. Ibid, 26.
7. Greg Ogden, *Transforming Discipleship: Making Disciples A Few At A Time* (Downers Grove, IL: InterVarsity Press, 2003), 69.
8. Ibid, 67.
9. Emory James, *The Small Church in the Mind of God: A Noumenological Perspective* (Orange, CA: ABM Publications, 2014).
10. Robert E. Coleman, *The Master Plan of Evangelism* (Grand Rapids, MI: Fleming H. Revell, 1993).

11. Kevin G. Harney, *Organic Outreach for Ordinary People: Sharing Good News Naturally* (Grand Rapids, MI: Zondervan, 2009).
12. Linda Bergquist & Allan Karr, *Church Turned Inside Out: A Guide for Designers, Refiners, and Re-Aligners* (San Francisco, CA: Jossey-Bass, 2010).

EPILOGUE

There are just some things that are done better on a small-scale, and discipleship is one of those things. Small-scale ministry is where the heart of discipleship happens. Small groups foster and cultivate environments for intimacy, authenticity, and vulnerability. It allows for imperfect people not only to have a place that is warm, welcoming and safe but one where the Spirit of grace has liberty to transform hearts and lives. These are environments where relational discipleship takes root and flourishes. It allows for a greater sense of interactive participation among all of its members. It becomes a place not only for individuals to belong but also to contribute. Relational discipleship happens most effectively on a small-scale level.

It is inevitable not to be involved in some form of small-scale ministry in your Christian lifetime. You will find yourself involved in some degree in some type of small-scale ministry. Whether you pastor or attend a small church, are involved in a small group at your large church, meet in an accountability group, counsel a pray for a friend, lead a ministry team at your church or a Bible study in your neighborhood or place of employment, you are a part of a small-scale ministry.

Knowing and understanding the dynamics involved in small-scale ministry is relevant towards greater leadership and discipleship efficacy. Considering the various perspectives and components that are at play in small-scale ministry will not only equip but also empower and inspire both leaders and the small groups they lead towards Great Commission fulfillment.

ABOUT THE AUTHOR

Bob DeSagun is a Christian educator, thinker, author, and speaker. He planted and pastors a small church in San Diego, California. He is a licensed and ordained minister with The Christian and Missionary Alliance where he has served in The South Pacific District's Executive Committee as well as their Licensing, Ordination, and Consecration Council. He serves as a leadership consultant for small churches. He is also an adjunct professor for Crown College in St. Bonifacius, Minnesota and serves as a trustee for Simpson University in Redding, California. He received his PhD from Regent University's School of Business and Leadership in Organizational Leadership with a major in Ecclesial Leadership. He and his wife Tina have been married for over 25 years and have a daughter Paige who has blessed them with their grandson Carter.

Made in the USA
Middletown, DE
10 November 2017